MW01272900

Acknowledgements:

There are three main groups of people I'd like to thank. mentors: Sonny Terry, Norton Buffalo, Charlie Musselwhit. Walter Horton, Tom Mazzolini, and many others. Secondly, my family and friends for their help and love. And thirdly, my students—those wonderfully patient and supportive 'guinea pigs'—for teaching me how to teach.

Dedication:

To that first generation of Blues People—most of whom are now playing their gigs on a higher plane. Also to T.J., C.G., V.V., and my other departed friends who are listening to them there.

Special Thanks to:

My beloved twin, Nina, for the 'Musical idiot' section. Dr. Charles Garfield, for his help on the 'Visualization' exercise. Steve Carillo, for his fine guitar work. Michael Starkman, David G. Williams, and Carol Barske for artwork. Melon Studios, for recording beyond the call of duty. Kevin and Richard for being the paste-up kings. Maryellen Sullivan-Hanley for calligraphy, and Rusty for watchin' the kids. My Mom, for buying me my first Harmonica. My Dad, for working harder than anyone ever should. Goldie and Max, my music-loving grandparents - and Rita.

Table of Contents

I hope that you will be using the taped part of this package at least as much, if not more, than the book. In fact, in a way you could consider this entire book to be a glorified table of contents for the tape!

You'll probably want to go through the book sequentially, as you listen to the appropriate recorded sections. So this Table of Contents will be minimal, and merely list the main sections of the book, along with those portions you will be most likely to want to look up for reference.

Introduction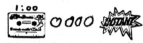

Hi! I'm Dave Harp, and I used to be a self-labeled 'Musical Idiot!' Didn't think I could even 'carry a tune in a bucket!' But now I love to play and teach the Blues Harmonica, and in the past 8 years I've taught more than 2000 people to Blow their Blues away in person, and nearly 10,000 more by book and cassette.

This is the 5th completely revised edition of my package, and I sincerely (if not modestly) believe that it's the most effective Blues Harmonica method available. Why? Because before I became the San Francisco Bay Area's only full-time Blues Harp teacher, my background was in psychology and experimental design. So I've tried to use each student of mine as a (pardon the expression) 'guinea pig,' and every group class as a 'controlled experiment' in order to develop the best and quickest way to teach Blues Harp. The end result of this extensive testing is in your hands right now.

This package may not be the world's greatest 'coffee table book' (unless you prefer useful rather than decorative things on your coffee table). In fact, my 5th edition is the first that I've bothered to have typeset, glossy covered and perfect bound (All the niceties beloved by those who judge their books by the cover). But if you'll give it, and yourself, half a chance — you could be playin' some Blues today! So load the cassette into your tape deck, read the following sections entitled "Zen and the Art of Blues Harp Blowing" and "How to Use This Package," then let's Blow! Why be a 'non-participant observer' or 'just a listener' if you love Music, the Blues, or Harmonica?!!

Zen and The Art of Blues Harp Blowing

Perhaps it does seem like a strange title - but it's **not** a joke. Because the psychological principles that underlie Zen and similar disciplines have recently been used to teach subjects as diverse as sports and drawing. Millions of people have learned new skills from books like "Inner Tennis," "Inner Skiing," and "Drawing on the Right Side of the Brain". And this same type of approach is exceptionally well-suited for the teaching of spontaneous, improvisational music such as Blues Harmonica!

The serious practitioners of Zen, Karate, Aikido, and Yoga often seem to possess nearly superhuman abilities. The best Zen archers can send an arrow straight to the target while blindfolded; the Karate and Aikido-Masters can disarm a dozen simultaneous attackers, and the top-of-the-line Yogis can voluntarily suspend pulse and respiration. The adept students of more 'Western' disciplines like self-hypnosis and 'superlearning' often perform the slightly less herculean tasks of quitting smoking or learning 1500 words of a foreign language in a single day. What have these strange but impressive feats to do with would-be Blues Harmonica players?

There are two main ways of playing music. One way is to use a notation system (such as the simple one I've developed for Harmonica) which tells us exactly when and what note to play. I call this mode of playing 'Classical' music. We are repeating note for note a piece of music which someone considered enough of a 'Classic' to write down. Most of us, unless we've already managed to convince ourselves that we are 'unmusical' or even 'tone-deaf' (in which case we **must** take the 'Musical Idiot' self-test first) can learn to 'pick out' a simple song like 'Twinkle Twinkle Little Star' from my notation within minutes.

The other way is to learn the wonderfully exciting way of making music known as **'improvising'. This involves creating the music second by second as we are playing it.** Improvising, or **Jamming,** is often done against a Blues backround provided by other musicians, although we can learn to do it alone as well.

When improvising, certain rules must be followed, but within these generalized rules the choice of notes is left to the player. Jamming can be one of the most freeing and self-expressive activities that you'll ever do in your life!

A Martial Arts Analogy

The student of Karate engages in two very different main types of training. On the technical level, he or she practices specific punches, kicks and blocks until they feel comfortable, natural, and familiar. He or she will also practice a mental state known as 'one-pointedness'. In this state, the student is relaxed but totally focused on the attacker, so that whichever offensive or defensive move is needed will flow naturally without need for mental analysis or self-criticism. Clearly, to criticise/analyze oneself in the midst of battle ("I should have kicked his kneecap and then...") would distract concentration from the necessities of the present situation. Zen and the other disciplines mentioned above also use approximately the same 'two-way' teachings to achieve their results (although the words used to label such teachings differ widely).

Improvisation: Locating the 'Mind's Ear'

Learning the ability to improvise music requires similar preparation. We must practice certain technical skills, rules, and guidelines, starting with a few very simple instructions and building up to the more technically demanding ones. At the same time (if we want to improvise rather than play Classical music) we'll have to begin to locate that mental state which Blues musicians refer to as: **'playing from the gut'** or **'playing with soul'**.

It's hard to describe that mental place in words. Some would say it's like being on 'automatic pilot' after you've learned to drive well. Others might say it's like the state you're in when you've danced so freely and wildly (probably after a few beers) that for just a few minutes you forgot to notice whether you were embarassing your partner or not! Perhaps it's even related to the way we can often begin a sentence without thinking - and the words just flow out, unplanned yet mostly making sense... But regardless of how we might verbalize it, the relaxation/visualization exercises on Page 90 will help you to get to that mental 'place' most condusive to creating music!

I've built certain 'high-tech' psychological teaching devices right into my package. Many of the recorded sections have **'subliminal suggestions'** (very softly recorded verbal instructions) to help you relax and not be critical of yourself while playing. Other teaching tools you'll have to use yourself. **Repetition** is one of them, as I'll describe further below, the **self-scoring 'Musical Idiot' test** is another, and the **visualization/relaxation exercise** is perhaps the most valuable.

But your most important task is to allow yourself a few hours of freedom from self-criticism as you first explore my book and cassette. Focus and concentrate on my written words, my voice, and the music. Don't permit those nagging, self-hating inner messages ("you can't do this - you're tone-deaf" or "you didn't understand that part right away? you must be dumb" etc.) to distract you. Give'em the day off! Most of my instructions are quite simple, and easily understood if you read or listen to them as many times as you need to, without 'self-sabotage!'

Even if you are a hard-headed, skeptical, non-believer in 'mystical' pursuits, these teaching techniques will work for you if you use them. However, enough pop-psychology for now. Continue on to the 'nuts-and-bolts' of this method, entitled 'How to Use this Package'.

How To Use This Package

Read this section through. Then relax, get comfortable, and try to set aside 90 minutes and listen to the entire tape. Glance at the book while listening to see how closely cassette and book correlate. **Notice that a small 'cassette logo' in the margin lets you know which portions of the book are illustrated on the tape.** To help you locate the appropriate taped portions when you're using the book, above each 'tape logo' I indicate the correct side of the cassette, and approximately how far along on that side the desired portion is. 00 means the very beginning of that side, 100 means the very end, and the little markers in the cassette 'reel window' will help you search. Remember, you don't have to try to play along right away, unless you want to.

Work with the book and tape at your own speed - that's what **'self-programming'** is all about. Listen to an entire section before beginning to try to play along with it.

Tape Deck Technique

Practice your **'Fancy Fast Fingering'**; you'll have to learn to hit those 'Fast Forward' and 'Rewind' buttons so as to hear a few seconds worth of tape over and over. Please don't be afraid to listen to a single piece of an exercise 5, 10 or as many times as you need to understand it and 'get the feel' of it - before you even put Harp to mouth!

If your deck has a 'counter' device, use the space provided next to the tape logo to write in what counter number each section begins on. I would have done this for you but each deck's counter is different. So run your cassette back to the very beginning, see where (The Introduction) I've written in '0000' for you (a good start), and begin to fill in some of the counter blanks in the book as you reach that section of the tape. Some students even like to write in a number for each exercise they are working on, to help them rewind and fast forward on that little chunk. So don't be afraid to write (neat and small, please) in the book.

How Long Will It Take?

How long 'should' it take you to master all of the information in this package? A few dedicated souls (who have usually at least 'fooled around a bit' with Harmonica already) will be able to do it in one tough, chap-lipped day. The 'average' beginner practicing from 15-45 minutes per day will complete the program in 2-6 weeks. Then, of course, Volume II beckons! In fact (hint hint) many of my Harp students have found that listening to Volume II while working with this first package was an excellent motivator. It also showed them exactly what they were working towards, even though they weren't as yet able to play quite that skillfully.

A Few More Hints

Everyone has a different approach to learning. Some are book oriented, and read each part of the book thoroughly before even turning to the tape. Others like to listen over and over to the tape, and don't even crack the book unless they are having a problem figuring out which notes are being used in an exercise (and need to look at my notation system while they listen). However, the clearest, fastest way to learn is with eye and ear co-ordinated. So, unless you are practicing while commuting, look at the notation or instructions for the song or exercise **while** you listen to it. But you know your own learning patterns best - so try to figure out an eye/ear balance that works best for you!

If you have ever considered yourself 'unmusical' or even 'tone-deaf', then the 'Musical Idiot' test is absolutely mandatory for you. If you never feel 'musically insecure', then you may be able to skip the 'Musical Idiot' section, although it's probably wise to skim it unless you're in a terrific hurry.

Instant Blues Harmonica

Are you interested **only** in Blues Improvisation; and not concerned with music theory, folk songs, 'Classical' music, or anything else clever that I might have to say? If so, you might want to use my '**Instant Harp**' format. This is a streamlined approach which avoids any 'extraneous' material. Just read the sections accompanied by the special '**Instant Harp Logo**,' and locate (use your counter, and mark the numbers down) and listen repeatedly to the appropriate tape portions. A few Instant Harp sections will not be illustrated on the tape. They too will be marked with an 'Instant Harp' logo. However, the 'Instant Harp' format will heavily emphasize use of the tape over use of the book.

If you have absolutely no experience with either Harmonica or Blues Music, you may find that the 'non-instant' complete book/tape program is more appropriate for you. Or feel free to try the 'instant' format, and refer back to the rest of the book or tape if you need more assistance.

Your first few hours of playing may seem frustrating, and like an 'uphill struggle', especially if you're a self-critical type of person. Cut yourself some slack at first - since a point of 'snowballing' returns will occur quickly. So don't discourage yourself, because:

The more you practice, the better you'll play.
The better you play, the more you'll enjoy playing.
The more you enjoy playing, the more you'll practice.

Archy the Cockroach and David Harp's Grammar

By the way: certain of you literarily-minded people may find it slightly strange that I occasionally change my 'pronoun persona'. But I prefer to use 'I' when I'm addressing you directly, as on the tape, and use 'We' when I'm discussing something that all of 'us harp-players' do. Besides, I'm a musician, not a pro grammarian! My rules regarding capitalization (Blues Harmonica?) are a bit eccentric also. But if e.e. cummings and archy the cockroach can get away with flexing the capital rules - at least I'm in good company!

How I Became An 'Ex-Musical Idiot!'

As a young child, I enjoyed singing and pretending to play along with records. But a few months of unwanted cello lessons at age 10 discouraged me from trying to make music for years, and convinced me of my 'tone-deafness'. I even took a certain 'macho' pride in being totally unmusical, and liked to joke about it ("I couldn't carry a tune with a handle on it"). However, when my high school friends started a little rock band in 1968, I desperately wanted to be in on the 'action'. Alas, by then everyone believed in my 'tone-deafness' and I was only allowed to carry equipment on stage and drunks off.

By 1969, after my first year in college, I decided to emulate my idol, Bob Dylan, by hitch-hiking to Alaska. I grew a scruffy beard (all that I could manage at the time) and bought a denim jacket, but something was missing from my costume... what was it? A Harmonica! And then I hit the road, Jack!

I was able to put my 'unmusical' self-image aside at that time for two reasons. Firstly, the late 1960's were a time of great change for me, so I was able to be somewhat flexible as I traded a 'macho' self-image for a more 'hippie-type' persona. Secondly, hitch-hiking gave me lots of time amongst people who didn't already 'know' me to be 'unmusical' (although some of my first rides quickly noticed my lack of virtuosity, and offered me the choice of shutting up or getting out.)

I'm glad now to say that I kept playing that first day, both during my rides and on the side of the road. After 13 or 14 lip-weary hours I picked out my tune number one, 'Blowin' in the Wind', from a Bob Dylan Harp songbook that I bought and brought with me. Being able to play even one song gave me confidence, and more good results followed quickly. The more I played, day by day, the more skillful my lips and ears became, and the better I sounded. And the better I sounded, the more I played. By the time I hit Vancouver, I could play a few songs well enough for my fellow travelers to really enjoy (the first few renditions, anyway...). Now, 15 years later, I love to play and teach the Blues Harp, and many other instruments!

Dr. N.S. Feldman, and the 'Musical Idiot' Syndrome

Dr. Nina S. Feldman is a Princeton-trained developmental psychologist whose skill in experimental design was sharply honed by her work at E.T.S. (Educational Testing Services is the designer of most of the nation's standardized tests.) Her fascination with the vagaries of human nature goes back even further, to when she first encountered her twin brother, David Harp!

3 years ago, Nina's expertise in the use of 'self-testing' as an educational tool combined with my interest in teaching music to people who considered themselves 'unmusical'. We devised a 35 question test and began administering it to self-described 'Musical Idiots' and 'Tonedeaf' folk. Analysis of the test results and interviews with our test subjects helped us to isolate what we consider to be the five main causes of musical blockage. A more complete book on the subject is in progress (inquiries welcome).

But that's enough family history - take it away, Nina!

9

Are You A Victim of the 'Musical Idiot' Syndrome?

How many times in the past few years have you found yourself envying a friend's or performer's musical abilities? Your train of thought may have been, "I wish **I** could play the piano like that", followed by, "I wish I could play **anything** like that", then, "I wish **I** could play anything!" and finally, "I guess I'm just not very musical".

Do you believe that these talented individuals had the privilege of being born with a natural musical ability? Or that they were 'made musical' by having been taught the secrets of music at an early age? Are you privately annoyed that your parents didn't start you on violin or piano lessons when you were five years old? Or perhaps a bit rueful because you did have childhood music lessons that somehow just didn't 'take'?

If your answer to any or all of these questions is "yes", then you may be a victim of the 'Musical Idiot" Syndrome. Being a 'Musical Idiot' simply means that, for whatever reasons, you perceive yourself as being underendowed with musical aptitude or ability. This self-perception has led you to abandon the pursuit of music, although the thought of someday learning to play an instrument is still an active part of your fantasy life. If the innermost recesses of your hall closet have ever harbored an unused harmonica or untuned guitar, it is time to raise your musical consciousness, clean out your closet, and bring those neglected instruments back into the light of day. Musical Idiots continue reading — help is on the way!

Self-Help For All

The decade of the '70's saw a tremendous upsurge of interest in the topic of self-improvement, as the 'Me' generation's childhood inadequacies were often resolved with a flourish. Your pear-shaped sixth grade buddy is now in training for the Boston Marathon. That painfully shy adolescent cousin is now a business executive and happily 'pulling her own strings'.

Unfortunately, most self-labeled 'unmusical' folk have not been able to apply these self-improvement techniques to their relationship with making music. This seems to be due to the fact that although an abundance of music instruction exists, the **root causes** of musical blockage remain largely unexplored. **For most musically unfulfilled adults, the problem is not a lack of instruction — it is a lack of belief in their own never-tapped musical ability.**

The following test is designed to explore your 'Musical Idiot' quotient. Though this test is not intended to predict how accomplished a musician you will become, it can help you understand and overcome the areas of musical blockage that have prevented you from realizing your own musical potential. There are no 'right' or 'wrong' answers in this test. Please answer as honestly as possible.

Your Musical I.Q.

1. Have you ever felt that it is 'too late' for you to be 'musical'?   yes/no

2. Have you ever bought yourself a musical instrument and then not **really** tried to learn to play it?

     yes   no, always tried to learn   no, never bought one

3. Do you ever look at people who can play some kind of instrument and wish that you had that type of talent?   yes/no

4. a) Did you take music lessons as a child?   yes/no
    b) Did you **want** to take music lessons as a child?   yes/no

5. Imagine yourself feeling an urge to sing. Will you sing:
    Only when alone in the shower or the car   Only with close friends, or when drinking
    No matter who else is present

6. In Elementary school music classes were:
    nonexistant / boring / enjoyable / difficult to understand / frightening
    (circle all that apply)

7. Have you ever fantasized about being able to play a musical instrument, even though you never actually tried to do it?   yes/no

8. Do you believe that most other people 'just kind of pick up' simple instruments like the harmonica by themselves?   yes/no

9. If someone placed an instrument in your hands and told you to 'make some sounds', would you feel:
    scared / pleased / foolish / excited / upset
    (circle any that apply)

10. If you saw an older adult taking beginning music lessons, would it strike you as:
    somewhat surprising? yes/no   somewhat inappropriate: yes/no

The diagnostic value of this test lies not in any total score (which you could use to compare to your friend's score, and brag or complain about) but in the five separate 'themes' that your answers will now help you to investigate. In this shortened version of the test, 2 questions relate to each of these five main areas of musical blockage. Please refer back to your answers to the designated questions as you read the following sections. Most people who believe that they are not 'musical' will find that at least a few of these problems apply directly to them.

The Myth of Innate Ability: Refer to Questions 3 and 8

Many people who foreclose on their own musical potential share a belief in a widespread and damaging musical myth. Do you believe that all musicians are born with innate musical talent? If the answer to this query is affirmative, you are wrong! **Musicians are made, not born!** A tremendous body of research exists to verify the fact that musical ability is a near-universal human characteristic that must be nurtured and encouraged.

Once you begin to **believe** this, you can leave your unmusical self-image behind. Vividly visualizing yourself playing the instrument of your choice will help you to end the negative habit of making self-deprecating 'tone-deaf' ("I couldn't carry a tune in a bucket") jokes. Though not all of us may have the energy, dedication or sensitivity to play just like a Pablo Casals or a Jimi Hendrix, the truth of the matter is that **anyone** with the sincere desire to be musical can learn to play a variety of instruments well.

Ageism: Refer to Questions 1 and 10

Ageism — that is, discrimination against a person based solely on the fact of biological age — is often practiced unconsciously by otherwise well-intentioned people. Prejudiced attitudes against the elderly have become a pervasive but often-unadmitted part of our culture. Ageist beliefs may be held by young and old alike, and directed either at others or oneself. Any person who may eye an untried activity and think wistfully, "I'm too old for that" is an unwitting victim of ageism. An ageist viewpoint holds that 'older' people are unlikely to continue to expore any existing talents and incapable of discovering new ones. Music is an ageless pastime! Any holding back that a non-musician might do based on this misguided belief is a sad and unneccessary loss of musical potential.

The next time you find yourself looking askance at the activities of an 'elderly' person who is taking some kind of lessons or engaging in a 'youthful' pastime, remember: that older adult may be **you** in 5, 10 or 40 years.

Noticing evidence that works **against** the ageist perspective (which is often promulgated by advertising and the media) such as senior citizens re-entering school or taking up a new sport or relationship may lighten your own response to the inevitable aging process.

Actress Billie Burke once remarked, "Age doesn't matter unless you're a cheese." Grandma Moses, Pablo Casals or Eubie Blake would surely agree!

Fear Of Foolishness: Refer to Questions 5 and 9

A major problem for many of the 'Musical Idiots' that have been tested is a preoccupation with the question: "What will people think?" Often a seeming fear of **failure** is actually a fear of **ridicule.**

If you find yourself feeling overwhelmed by social conventions as you start to play an instrument, or even think of playing, take a moment to look at what is causing these negative feelings. Ask yourself two very important questions: "If I were alone for two months to do as I pleased, how would I really feel about pursuing this?" And, "How do I think **other people** would react to my doing this?" You may find that you are drawn to learning, but fear that others would disapprove. If this is the case, take a few seconds to answer one additional question, "If not now, WHEN?", and then decide whether to follow your own feelings, or your imagined perceptions of other's reactions.

Early Musical Exposure: Questions 4 and 6

Your early music exposure may shape the rest of your musical...or, non-musical career. A bad first experience with music may create lasting difficulties. Some of the following are common problems that precipitate a negative attitude towards music. Did your parents force you to take music lessons? Did Mr. Flutesnoot's music class make your Tuesday mornings miserable throughout grade school? If so, you may not be willing to embark on a relationship with any other music teacher. Did an unkind comment on your early playing embarrass you away from further musical self-exposure? Parents, peers, and teachers play an important role in supporting an early love of music. Attitudes towards music will flourish if a child is first exposed in a supportive and involving manner. But, the converse is also true. Early discouragement will carry a tremendous impact on a young person's future musicality.

Understanding the effects that early encouragement and discouragement have on you is a crucial part of relinquishing a 'Musical Idiot' status. As you peruse your past, tell yourself **"What's past is over — unless I let it influence me now. Today, in the present, I can change my self-image and begin to be musical!"** The irascible Mr. Trebleclef from 4th grade has been retired for years, and it's time to get on with business — the business of bringing music into your life!

Approach/Avoidance: Refer to Questions 2, 7 and 9

These questions can indicate the presence of a common psychological conflict known as approach (wanting very much to be muscial) avoidance (fearful of making an attempt to do so). Buying a musical instrument is a strong statement of approach, as is fantasizing about playing. If you do these things but then do not follow through by actually learning to make music, you may be in the grip of a very strong musical approach/avoidance process. Sometimes the existence of an approach/avoidance conflict can produce very strong feelings, so if your answer to question 9 included the feelings of 'scared' or 'upset', or especially combinations like 'scared/excited', you may have an approach/avoidance attitude towards music. Acknowledging an ambivalence towards music can be the first step towards understanding how this conflict came about.

Bringing Music Into Your Life

The most common general causes of 'being unmusical' are found amongst the five problem themes described above. **No longer can you avoid the real issues by merely saying, "I guess I'm just Tone-deaf", since no such disease actually exists! If you can hear, you can be musical! There is only one valid reason for your non-musicality: lack of effort or practice!**

The only thing that now stands between you and your music is the time and energy necessary to accomplish whatever musical goal you've set for yourself. Furthermore, attributing your current lack of musicality to a lack of **effort** rather than a lack of **ability** offers you the option of becoming musical **whenever** you **choose** to put the effort into doing so. If your goals are realistic ("I will begin to play some guitar" rather than "I must play like Andre Segovia" or "I will take up Blues Harmonica" rather than "I must play avante-garde jazz oboe") then your success is virtually guaranteed from the outset. All that is necessary is to find a competent and empathetic teacher or a well recommended beginner's self-teaching method and you'll be on your way!

Which Harp to Buy and Why

There are a number of models and brands of Harmonicas that are appropriate for playing Blues. These 'Blues-style' Harps all have 10 holes, are all tuned to produce a 'Major Scale' (I'll explain this on pages 27 and 28 if you're interested), and range in price between $5.00 and $15.00. Each is tuned to a particular 'key' (page 28). The concept of 'key' is somewhat theoretical, but all you **need** to know about key now is that each Harmonica has a little letter, like 'C' or 'F', stamped into its cover. Each different key (letter) sounds just slightly different from the other ones.

I've chosen to make my tape using a key of 'F' Harp, so if you want to play along with me and sound the same you'll need an 'F' also. You can use another key Harp, but it will be a lot more difficult and less satisfying, and you won't be able to play along with my guitar music. So I STRONGLY advise you to obtain an 'F' (see my offer on back page). It really is the best Harp to learn on. I know, because I've tried them all out on my students!

Unfortunately, the most popular key sold is 'C' which happens to be the **worst** possible choice for the beginning Blues Harpist, due to the fact that a crucial note is very hard to obtain on a 'C' Harp. Once you learn to play your 'F', however, the 'C' will be easy to master. But **don't** start out on it.

My favorite brand and model is the Hohner 'Golden Melody' ($11.50 list price) available at any good music store. But any 10 hole 'F' Harmonica is OK to use with this package. The Huang brand 'Silvertone Deluxe' or 'Star Performer' models are excellent low cost (around $6.00) alternatives for your first Blues Harp.

What's Easy and What's Hard?

That's a good question, and not simple to answer. Some of you may have problems in keeping track of whether you are sucking in or blowing out, others will have great lung control but erratic rhythm. For this reason, you should probably take a 'shotgun' approach and try many different styles of playing rather than spending a long time trying to master any particular piece that seems difficult. Here are a few general hints:

Anything involving single notes will be hard at first. So don't obsess about obtaining single notes, just use 'Chords' (wide mouth). Aim in the general area of the note you want, but don't be too perfectionistic about exact location or you may lose your rhythm.

The better that you already know a song, the easier it will be to play. So look at my notated folk songs, and if you know and like one, try to play it from the notation.

If you are somewhat familiar with Blues music, the improvisational Sections XI, XII, and XIII may have parts that will be easy for you. If you haven't listened to Blues music very much yet, listen lots to all the music sections on the tape.

Almost everyone finds the simple train, Section IV, easy. It's not quite a Blues, but it's fun to play, and a great lung exercise.

If you're a 'nuts and boltsy' kind of person, and the 'theoretical approach' leaves you cold, try to read and listen to the theory chapter, but don't get stuck there. It's optional, anyways.

Lastly, do the Relaxation/Visualization Exercise, with or without Harp. It really will help you!

Section I: Meet Your Harp

Most of the information in Section I is contained in the tape. Pictured here is the most popular 'pre-wah wah' method of holding the harp (for righties). **However, almost any way of holding the harp that feels comfortable is OK.**

Listen to my discussion of 'chords' and 'dischords' on Harp, Piano and Guitar. Hearing about them will tell you a lot more than reading about them. Learn to play the low chord composed of holes number one, two, and three blow, so that we can check your tape deck speed.

Now is a good time to practice your inhaling (Suck) and exhaling (Blow) on the low end of your Harp. Really focus on your breathing, and think 'Suck' as you inhale and 'Blow' as you exhale until you are certain that you know which is which every time!

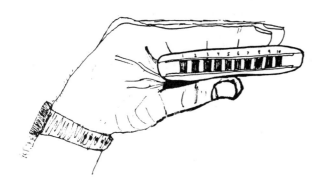

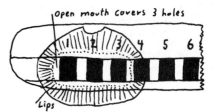

open mouth covers 3 holes

Lips

Tape Deck Speed

Hopefully your tape deck plays at the correct speed, so that your low blow chord sounds like mine. If your low blow chord sounds more like my "E" chord, then your tape deck is fast and you may want to buy an "F sharp" Harp to play with the tape. If your low chord sounds more like my "F sharp" chord, then your tape deck is slow and you may want to buy an "E" Harp. If none of these chords sound similar to your 1, 2, and 3 Blow chord, you might consider buying a new tape deck (most new decks play at the correct speed). The cheapest 'Radio Shack' model costs about $20 and is quite adequate. You can work with an off-speed deck if you must, but it will be a lot more difficult and less satisfying; rather like playing with the wrong key Harmonica. You'll sound fine on your solo pieces, but 'out-of-tune' when playing with the deck.

If you can't tell whether your sound matches the tape's sound, it probably does. Just start working with the package, and your ears will become more confident and competent as you practice. Then after a few hours or days return to this chord comparison, and your fine-honed ears will be able to judge your tape deck's tuning!

Optional Music Theory Chapter for the Musical Idiot

You don't have to understand music theory in order to make music. But many of my students have found that understanding the 'underpinnings' of music has helped them both in their playing and in their appreciation for the process involved in the art of music. So read this chapter (unless it seems really threatening; it is optional) but **don't get 'hung up' here.**

I do understand that if you got your first and only dose of music education in your local grammar school then you probably: A) Don't know very much about music theory (at least not any more) and B) Might feel intimidated by the very idea of music theory. So I'll try to make my explanations as simple and palatable as possible.

All sounds are caused by vibrations. Think about this - if we throw a stone into the middle of a pond of still water, ripples will spread out from the stone's point of impact. If there is a leaf floating at the edge of the pond, soon the ripples will reach it, and make the leaf move up and down, at the same speed as the ripples.

Whenever we vibrate the tiny metal "reed" (see Open Harp Surgery, P. 94) inside our Harp by blowing it, or pluck a guitar string, or clap our hands - we create vibrations that float through the air until they reach a sensitive membrane inside our heads called the eardrum. The eardrum (rather like our floating leaf) then vibrates at exactly the same speed as the vibrating metal reed, the guitar string, or the flesh of our clapping hands. Our brain then interprets these vibrations as a 'sound'. **The faster the vibrations the higher the sound. The slower the vibrations the lower the sound.** A mosquito's wings vibrate very rapidly, and a bullfrog's throat vibrates very slowly. The human brain can "hear" or "interpret" vibrations from a low of 20 vibrations per second to a high of about 20,000 vibrations per second (let's abbreviate vibrations per second as V.P.S.)

Most musically untrained people think of sound in a rather vague and linear way. A sound is either 'high' or 'low'. A picture of their mental 'sound-view' might look like this:

Very Low | Bullfrog | Big Motorcycle no muffler | Mans' Voice | Boys' Voice | Girls' Voice | Small dog yapping | Mosquito | Very High

But in reality, sounds are arranged in 'repeated cycles'. What does that mean? I'll try to explain it clearly and simply.

There is one more crucial fact that we must learn about the vibrations that create sound. Let's take any particular vibrational speed which produces a sound, 200 V.P.S. for example. If we compare this particular sound, or 'note' with the note produced by 400 V.P.S. (exactly twice as fast), we'll find that the two sounds seem remarkably alike, although the 'faster-vibration' sound is obviously higher. If we double the speed of vibration once again (800 V.P.S.), we find that all 3 sounds (200, 400 and 800 V.P.S.) bear a great similarity to each other. Likewise the sounds produced by 300 V.P.S., 600 V.P.S. and 1200 V.P.S., sound alike, and so on. **Doubling the speed of vibration of a particular sound will always produce a new sound that is very similar to the first one, only higher. We call these similar notes 'OCTAVE' notes. We can also call the 'distance' between two Octave notes 'One Octave'.**

Most people can immediately hear the similarity of these Octave notes. In fact, if you train your dog to expect food when he hears a sound of 200 V.P.S., he'll drool for a tone of 400 V.P.S. as well! If we refer to the sound produced by 200 V.P.S. as our first Octave note, then 400 V.P.S. will be called our second Octave note, and so on. We might picture this as a 'Cyclic Arrangement', rather similar in some ways to the arrangement of the calendar. We'll demonstrate this for ourselves with our Harps (P. 57).

Before calendars were invented, most people probably had a very vague and linear sense of time, rather like the non-musician's sense of sound.

Too far back to remember ___ A while ago ___ Right now ___ Soon after ___ Much later on

Yet the passage of time can actually be described or labeled more clearly if we think of it in terms of a 'repeated cycle'. Think about it!

You see, January '83 is quite like January '84, even though they are separated by one 'natural cycle'. And January '85 is still similar to January '83 and January '84. And April '83, April '84 and April '85 are quite alike in character, just as 250 V.P.S., 500 V.P.S. and 1000 V.P.S. are similar in sound. Recognizing the existence of these cycles (instead of thinking about them in 'vague and linear' terms) and labeling them makes it easier to describe, and use, the natural phenomenons of time and sound.

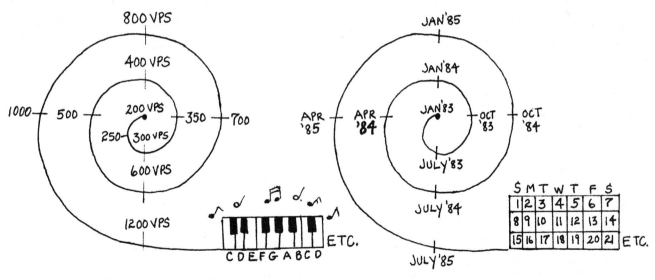

Repeated Sound Cycle   Repeated Time Cycle

Music History for the Musical Idiot

One of humankind's earliest musical instruments was the hunting bow. Some ancestral huntsman or huntswoman realized one day that the 'plunk' sound of the bowstring changed when the bow string was stretched more tightly or loosely. Many aboriginal peoples still use the bow to make music today. They simply place one end of the bow on the ground, and lean on the top end of the bow to stretch or loosen the bowstring as they pluck it. The effect is somewhat like a one-stringed bass fiddle, or 'washtub bass'.

2500 years ago the Greek Metaphysician Pythagoras turned his brilliant mind to the question of why the bow string produced different sounds when stretched and unstretched. He then discovered that lengths of string stretched between two points with equal tension would produce varying sounds depending on the length of the string.

Pythagoras began to experiment with the sounds produced by plucking different lengths of string. He soon noticed that if he plucked two strings simultaneously when one was exactly twice as long as the other, they would both produce sounds that somehow seemed very similar, even though the shorter string made a sound that was clearly higher.

Half as long
Twice as fast

Twice as long
Half as fast

We now know that the 'half-as-long' string was vibrating exactly twice as fast as the longer string, and thus the shorter string was producing a second Octave note which sounded very much like the longer string's first Octave note. But the vibrational nature of sound was not discovered until nearly 1700 A.D., so Pythagoras had only the relative lengths of the strings to base his research on. He reasoned that if the mathematical 'ratio' of 2 to 1 (one string twice as long as the other) would produce two sounds that seemed so similar, perhaps other simple ratios like 3 to 2 or 4 to 3 could be applied to the lengths of vibrating strings to produce more sounds that somehow 'related well' to each other.

Pythagoras continued his experimentation. He stretched some convenient length of string out, and plucked it to produce his first Octave note. He then plunked his finger down exactly in the middle of the string, which created two lengths of string, each exactly one-half as long as the original. Each of these new 'half-length' strings produced a second Octave note when plucked. He then used a variety of simple mathematical ratios (like 5 to 4, 3 to 2, 4 to 3 etc.) to decide how he wanted to divide up these second Octave lengths of string. Eventually he ended up by dividing each string into 12 equal sections. Why did he do it just this way? No one today knows for sure, but a quick look at a modern guitar or piano will clearly show that Pythagoras' 12 note Octave division has stood the test of time!

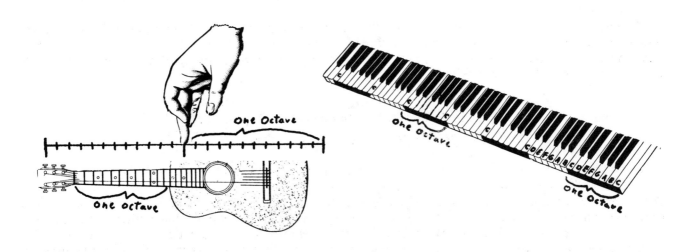

Pythagoras' Chromatic Scale

We call this process of breaking up the Octave distance into a number of smaller pieces 'creating a scale'. The word 'scale' refers to some particular way of dividing that Octave distance into pieces. **Pythgoras' 12 note division** (actually a 13 note division if you count the first and last note of the scale which are really the 'same' notes, one Octave apart) **is called the CHROMATIC SCALE. It is still the basic scale used by most of our Western civilization's music and musical instruments.**

Look at the 12 note Chromatic Scales built into the Piano and the Guitar. On the guitar, a series of ridges (called 'Frets') allow each string to be easily divided up into 12 parts by pressing a finger behind a particular Fret. The string is then only able to vibrate from that 'fingered' Fret to the bottom of the guitar.

The physical structure of the piano demonstrates its use of the Chromatic Scale even more clearly than that of the guitar. A piano contains 6 or 8 Chromatic Scales placed next to each other. By the late middle ages each piano note had been assigned a letter name. The white notes are indicated by a simple letter (C—E—F—G—A—B—C), but each black note has two names. The black note between the white notes C and D, for instance, can called either C# (C-Sharp, meaning 'higher than C') or Db (D-Flat, meaning 'lower than D'). Same exact note, two names.

If music theory is interesting to you, read off each letter name on the piano from any C note to the next highest. Notice that in one Octave I've used the b (Flat) names for each black note, and in another Octave I've used all # (sharp) names. We usually consider the Chromatic Scale to run from C to C, although it would be perfectly correct to read or play a Chromatic Scale from an Eb to Eb, or from A# to A#, or any other possible combination, as long as it began and ended with the same note. **Scales always begin and end on the same note, one Octave apart!**

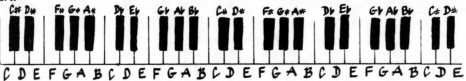

The Major Scale, The Minor Scale, and the Blues Scale

Many different types of scales exist, and each scale is used to create a different kind of music. In a way, **we might consider a scale to be a kind of "musical alphabet".** By using various combinations of the 26 letters of the English alphabet we create English words, sentences, paragraphs and books. By using the letters of the Russian alphabet we create Russian words, sentences, and long, dreary novels. Likewise, the notes of any particular culture's scale, be it a Greek scale, a Chinese scale, or a Martian scale, can be put together in various combinations to create music with a sound characteristic of that culture.

Although Pythagoras' Chromatic Scale is the basis of Western civilization's music, it is rarely used in its complete 12 note form. Instead, certain notes are chosen from it (usually 7) to form what we might consider 'child' scales from their 12 note ' mother'. Each of these 'child' scales has a particular sound or feel of its own. To continue with my musical alphabet analogy, we could consider these 'child' scales as 'dialects' which come from a 'mother' tongue, just as the Southern drawl, Yankee twang, or Cockney accents are delightfully different but derivative ways of speaking 'mother' English. Many scales of this type were experimented with after Pythagoras' death. By the Middle Ages, two of these 'child' scales had become far more popular than any of the others that had been tried. **These two most popular scales were named the MAJOR and MINOR scales.** Each has 8 notes and begins and ends on the same (octave) note (so there are really only 7 different notes in each scale). But the way that each scales's octave distance is broken up is different. Thus the Major and Minor scales have very different 'feels' to them. **The Major Scale eventually evolved as the basis for much of Northern and Western Europe's music.** We might even call it the 'musical alphabet' for most German and English 'Classical' music. **It tends to have a strong, Brassy, Bouncy feel to it.** Even random playing of the Major Scale notes sounds good to us - because these notes are the most basic building blocks of our American musical heritage. The Minor Scale evolved as the basis for much of Eastern Europe's music. It has a more plaintive or wistful quality, and we might consider it to be the 'alphabet' of most Gypsy, Yiddish, and European 'Folk-Style' music.

We can begin a Major or Minor scale on any note, then choose the rest of the appropriate scale notes from the 'mother' Chromatic Scale. And of course, by definition, we will end our scale on the same note (one octave higher) that we began on. The letter name of that first and last note then identifies the scale. So a Major Scale starting and ending on the note 'D' is called a 'D Major' Scale, a Minor Scale beginning on B-Flat (Bb) is called a 'Bb Minor Scale', and so on. The 'key' of a song refers to the beginning note of the scale used to play that song. **Your 'F' harp (invented by Mr. Hohner, a German) was set up to produce an F Major Scale most easily.** All of The Major Scale songs on pages 36 through 40 will then be in the key of F.

There is one more 'Musical Alphabet' that we must learn about: **The AFRO — AMERICAN BLUES SCALE!** **These 6 notes chosen from The Chromatic Scale** (7 notes if we count the last one, which is the same as the first) **will always sound 'BLUESY' when played together in any combination.** We'll listen, and learn, much more about The Blues Scale in Section IX. You might want to see how The Major, Minor, and Blues Scale compare with each other. Since all three are chosen from the original Pythagorean Chromatic Scale notes, this chart below will show which Chromatic notes are used and which ones left out to form each of these scales. We know that a Scale can be begun on any note, but I'll use 'C' as my beginning point since **we will be playing a 'C' Blues Scale on our 'F' harps (as explained in Section III). This means that we will be playing our Blues 'in the key of C.'**

"C" Chromatic Scale :	C	Db	D	Eb	E	F	Gb	G	A♮	A	Bb	B	C	(13 notes from "C" to "C")
"C" Major Scale :	C	✕	D	✕	E	F	✕	G	✕	A	✕	B	C	(8 notes from "C" to "C")
"C" Minor Scale :	C	✕	D	Eb	✕	F	✕	G	Ab	✕	Bb	✕	C	(8 notes from "C" to "C")
"C" Blues Scale :	C	✕	✕	Eb	✕	F	Gb	G	✕	✕	Bb	✕	C	(7 notes from "C" to "C")

Single Notes

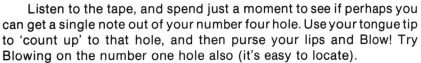

Listen to the tape, and spend just a moment to see if perhaps you can get a single note out of your number four hole. Use your tongue tip to 'count up' to that hole, and then purse your lips and Blow! Try Blowing on the number one hole also (it's easy to locate).

Remember to use the tip of your tongue to check that you're centered on a hole, and make sure that the Harmonica is contacting the wet inner membrane of your lips - not the dry outer part. The upper lip should be well over the Harp and the lower lip well under it.

Your lips are 'pouted out', so that your upper lip is almost trying to touch your nose. Think about how your lips feel when you whistle, or try to drink a very thick milkshake through a straw. 'Protrude' them out, don't Suck'em in for the best possible fit. Get used to the feeling of the musculature **all around** the lips protruding them outwards to form a small, circular hole (use a mirror here to see what I mean). **Lips pout out, Harp pushes in against them. You should feel a tension in the corners of your mouth as you eat (put it way in there) that 'tin sandwich'. But try to keep your tongue and throat relaxed, even though your lips are tense.**

Single notes seem hard? They'll come - just aim at the single hole you want, and use chords for now! There is one other way to obtain single notes (called 'tongue-blocking') but it's not too useful for Blues. If you already can 'tongue-block', practice the above method as well.

Timing

No sense in reading about this, folks - it's easier to learn from the tape. Practice tapping and saying 'one-two-three-four' as I do. I'll discuss the 'hoof n' mouth' problem in detail later on.

David's Harptab™ Notation System and the Major Scale

If I were a 'regular' music teacher I would now require you to learn the complicated but widespread system of musical notation known as 'Standard Notation'. I would write down all of my songs in 'Standard', and if you found it hard to learn you'd just be out of luck!

And if all of the instructions for the game of volleyball were in French, you'd have to learn French before you could engage in a friendly game of volleyball.

Well, playing volleyball is much easier than learning French, and playing Harmonica is much easier than learning Standard Notation. Therefore I'll just show you my own amazingly simple Harmonica notation system, and we'll begin to play right away!

B means Blow. S means Suck. The number written (1 through 10) indicates which hole (notice the little numbers stamped onto your Harp) to use. A dot indicates when the beat falls, that is, exactly when your foot hits the floor. Any special directions will be written above the notation.

So my Major Scale with countdown looks like this: read it while you listen.

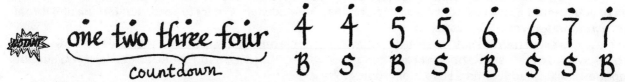

You can play it either single note or chordally. Do get the feel of this scale, even if you can't single note it. Practice your tape deck technique; rewind and play, rewind and play....

You'll find that if you listen to the next few songs while you read their Harptab™ notations (Twinkle Twinkle Little Star and Beethoven's Ode to Joy), my 'voice-over' instructions will help to make the notation system perfectly clear to you.

Locating the Right Holes

At first, the temptation is to try to locate a particular hole by keeping your eyes on the little numbers on the cover plate. This will rapidly drive you cross-eyed, however, and as the Harp approaches your mouth too closely you can no longer see the numbers. So let's drop that method right now!

Fortunately, the mouth is one of the most sensitive and 'fast-learning' organs of the body. This is because a large portion of the brain is devoted to operating the mouth (although hearing certain people talk may make you disbelieve that fact). Your lips will quickly 'learn' where each hole is with a few days practice. At first, however, you may need to 'count holes' with your tongue-tip to make sure that you are on the desired one. Or you can find a particular hole by holding your Harp between the tips of your thumb and forefinger, with your forefinger tip exactly over the hole that you want. Then just touch your forefinger to the center of your upper lip and presto! There you are!

Learning the Distance Between Holes

The distance between the center of one hole and the center of the next is approximately 5/16 of an inch (that helps a lot, doesn't it). Just a touch of practice with the Major Scale, or even with two adjacent notes like the one blow and two blow will teach you to 'feel' that distance in your hand and mouth. Play one blow - three blow - one blow. It really is quite a different movement. We'll practice these 'distance jumps' more with our next song - it really is easy!

Why I Use 'Those' Words

I'm afraid that a few of you may have slight negative feelings about my use of the words 'Suck' and 'Blow'. Therefore I'd like to explain exactly why I use them.

It wasn't a casual decision, and I certainly didn't do it to 'bug' people. I tried 'Inhale' and 'Exhale' (too long to fit in quickly). I tried 'Draw' and 'Push' (people just didn't **relate** to them as quickly as to Suck and Blow). 'In' and 'Out' almost worked, but were difficult to hear clearly in combination with certain numbers ('seven-in?'). So after much thought, I decided to stick with 'Suck' and 'Blow'.

Many words in our language have more than one meaning, and once we're accustomed to the 'non-offensive' usage we never even think about it. No one could object to the sentence "The dam has broken!" even though the same-sounding word used as an expletive might offend many. Likewise, the name of a popular dice game; or the word describing our most commonly used type of spiral-shaped fastening device also happen to double as 'off-color' words. But we say these words often enough in their 'normal' usages so that no one thinks twice about it!

'Suck' and 'Blow' are the words that **work best** for people learning to play the Harmonica. And you'll find that after just a few minutes of listening to my tape - you'll be so accustomed to the **legitimate** use of these terms that they won't seem the slightest bit strange anymore!

Articulation

Practice saying **'tah'** as you listen to my description of the proper tongue position. Feel that 'Tongue-Dam' burst and the 'Tah' explode out!

Chord Notation

We form a chord by playing the note on **either side** of the note that is the name note of the chord. In other words, the four blow chord is composed of three blow, four blow, and five blow!

$$\text{Single note } 4 \text{ becomes Chord } \underline{345}; \quad 2 \text{ becomes } \underline{123}; \quad 4 \text{ becomes } \underline{345}$$
$$ B B \; S S S S$$

You don't need much technical expertise to play using chords. Just aim for approximately the middle note of the chord you desire, mouth open wide, and make sure you know whether to Blow or Suck. You'll be at least moderately 'right-sounding' most of the time!

Articulation Practice

Work with the four blow note or chord for awhile. Concentrate on the timing as you work with the tape, and avoid actually **vocalizing** the 'tah' (whisper it). Try tahing other notes, too, and keep those beats of silence silent! Don't Suck your air back **through** the Harp and risk a sound during a beat of silence. Tahs on four blow:

Keep silent beats silent! (Silence is Golden)

Tah Tah Tah
4 4 4 .
B B B Breathe

Tah Tah Tah
4 4 4 .
B B B Breathe

Tah Tah Tah
4 4 4 .
B B B Breathe

Mouth Only Breathing

Become aware of how you can open or close the connection between nose and mouth that exists at the back of your throat. Not sure that you can? Then practice breathing through your nose only, but with your mouth open. It should feel as though the back of your tongue is 'pushed up' as you do this. Now breathe through your mouth only, without leaking any air from your nose. It's easy to do when you concentrate on it.

You will usually want to channel all the air through your mouth and your Harp (unless you prefer to play through a nostril - it can be done and is useful in discouraging others from asking to play your Harps).

Sucking Articulations

Blowing articulations like 'tah' through your Harp is easy-it's just like talking. but those Suck articulations are tougher. When we talk, we take a good deep breath (inhale) and then proceed to 'talk it out', to exhale in a slow and controlled manner with lots of articulation then we grab another quick inhale, and again release it in words. Conversely, **we harpists must often inhale slowly and controlledly with articulations, then rapidly expel our air to prepare for another long, slow, articulated inhalation. Learing to do this is good for our lungs and diaphragm as well as our playing! So practice!** And really, try just a bit of inhale talking - just start out with empty lungs and hold your nose shut. When will we ever stop having fun?

Tahs on four Suck (empty lungs during silent beats):

one two three four
Tah 345 S, Tah 345 S, Tah 345 Breathe, Tah 345 S, Tah 345 S, Tah 345 Breathe, Tah Tah Tah 444 S S S Breathe, Tah Tah Tah 444 S S S Breathe

34

Breathe during the silences (if you need to) when Sucking and Blowing on the four hole:

one two three four 4 4 4 . 4 4 4 . 4 4 4 . 4 4 4 .
S S S   B B B   S S S   B B B

Tahing the Major Scale:

one two three four
Tah Tah Tah Tah Tah Tah Tah Tah
4 4 5 5 6 6 7 7
B S B S B S S B

Don't spend too much time on these above exercises. Some of the actual songs below are easier to play than the Major Scale, and rather more satisfying musically as well.

Playing Major Scale Type Songs on Our Harmonicas

Look for songs you know well in the only complete Major Scale, using holes 4,5,6, and 7. The Major Scales found between holes 1 through 4 and holes 7 through 10 are missing certain notes. Mr. Hohner had to arrange the notes this way so that we would get good-sounding chords no matter where we Blow or Suck.

Your "F" Harp

Hole #	1	2	3	4	5	6	7	8	9	10
Suck notes	G	C	E	G	B♭	D	E	G	B♭	D
Blow notes	F	A	C	F	A	C	F	A	C	F

"F" Major Scale
FGAB♭CDEF

"Twinkle Twinkle Little Star" is our first real song! Practice that four blow to six blow jump for a moment, listen to the song while reading the notation a few times, then 'go for it!' Add some articulations once you're comfortable with it and perhaps a few 'wah-wahs' as well.

Twinkle	Twinkle	Little	star	How	I	wonder	what	you	are
4 4	6 6	6 6	6	5	5	5 5	4	4	4
B B	B B	5 5	B	5	5	B B	5	5	B

Up	a	bove	the	world	so	high	Like	a	teacup	in	the	sky
6	6	5	5	5	5	4	6	6	5 5	5	5	4
B	B	5	5	B	B	5	B	B	5 5	B	B	5

Twinkle	Twinkle	Little	star	How	I	wonder	what	you	are
4 4	6	6	6 6	6	5	5	5 5	4	4	4 (Ahem!)
B B	B	B	5 5	B	5	5	B B	5	5	B

The Hand 'Wah-Wah'

Use any hand position that allows you to form a 'cup' in back of your Harp that can be open and shut. This is similar theoretically to the so-called 'war whoop' produced by flapping your palm in front of your mouth while yelling. The hand wah wah is expecially useful as a tone enhancer on notes held more than one or two beats.

Wrists stay together

Right hand Fingers Open + close the 'cup'

36

Downbeats and Upbeats

In my notation system, a dot ● indicates the downbeat, and an 'umbrella' ⌒ **indicates what occurs during the upbeat.**

one two three four Down Up Down Up Down Up Down DUDUDUD DUDUDUD

Practice tapping your foot and observing the downbeats and upbeats while saying your new **Tuka** articulation.

Down Up Down Up Down Up
Tuka Tuka Tuka *Breathe* Tuka Tuka Tuka *Breathe* Tuka Tuka Tuka *Breathe*

Now try **Beethoven's Ninth Symphony (the "Ode to Joy")**. Play it chordy, rich and slow. It's very easy, but in a few places you must play two notes in one beat. Listen while reading the Harptab™ a few times before playing.

one two three four 5 5 6 6 5 5 4 4 4 5 5 4 5 5 6 6 5 5 4 4 4 5 4 4
B S B S B S B B S B B S B S B B S B S B B S B S B

4 5 4 4 5 5 5 4 4 5 5 4 4 4 3 5 5 6 6 5 5 4 4 4 4 5 4 4 4
S B B S B S B S B S B B S B S B B S B B S B S B B S B S B B

Old Favorite Major Scale Songs

"Oh When The Saints Go Marching In": Try some wah-wahs on the longer held notes-play it fast for a party, slow for a funeral.

Oh when the saints go marchin in   Oh when the saints go marchin in
4 5 5   6   4 5 5 6   4 5 5   6 5 4 5 4
B B B   B   B B B B   B B B   B B B B B

yes I want to be in that number   When the saints go marchin in
5 4 4 4 5 6 6 6 5   5 5 6   5 4 4 4
B B B B B B B B B   B B B   B B B B

"Michael Row The Boat Ashore": Notice that some notes fall on the up beats, so watch your foot as you play (and keep that foot-beat **steady**).

Michael row the boat a shore Halley loooo yah Michael row the boat a shore Halley loo hoo yah
4 5 6 5 6 6 6   5 6 6 6   5 6 6 6   5 5 5 4 4 4 4
B B B B B B B   B B B B   B B B B   B B B B B B B

Jor dan river is deep and wide Hall ey loooo yah Milk and honey on the other side Halley loo hoo oo hoo yah
4 5 6 6 5 6   6 6   7 7 6 6 5   5 6 6 6 5 5 5 5 4 4 5 4 4
B B B B B B   B B   B B B B B   B B B B B B B B B B B B B

38

"Row Row Row Your Boat": Three notes occur during one beat in a few places.

Row Row Row your boat gently down the stream.

4	4	4	4	5	5	4	5	5	6
B	B	B	5	B	B	5	B	5	B

Merrily Merrily Merrily Merrily life is but a dream

7 7 7	6 6 6	5 5 5	4 4 4	6	5	5	4	4
B B B	B B B	B B B	B B B	B	5	B	5	B

"Taps": Play it slowly at dusk with lots of hand wah-wah. Inhale quickly, between beats.

Day is done   night's begun.

3 3 4   3 4 5   3 4 5 3 4 5 3 4 5 4 5 6 5 4 3 3 3 4 *fade out*

B B B   B B B   B B B B B B B B B B B B B B B B B B B B B

"Reveille": Play it loudly and jauntily at first light, to enliven your fellow campers.

3 4 5 4 3   3 4 5 4 3   3 4 5 4 3 4 5 4   3 4 5 4 3   3 4 5 4 3   3 4 5 4 3 3 4 .

B B B B B   B B B B B   B B B B B B B B B   B B B B B   B B B B B   B B B B B B B

5 5 5 5 6 5 4 5 4 5 4 5 4   5 5 5 5 6 5   4 5 4 3 3 1

B B B B B B B B B B B B B   B B B B B B B   B B B B B B (repeat line one)

39

"Silent Night": Songs learned young, come back easily!

Si i lent night Ho oly night all is calm all is bright Round yon virg ir gin mother and child
6 6 6   5   6 66 5   4   4   3   4   4   6   6   6   7   7 6   6   6   6   5
B 5 B   B   B 5 B B   5   5   5   B   B   B   5   5   B   5   5   B   5   B   B

Ho ly in fant so tender and mild sleep in hea ven ly pe ee ace Sleep in hea ven ly pe e e ace
6 6   7   7   6   6 6 6 6   5   4   4   5   4   3   4 3 4 5   7   6   5   6   5   4 4 3 2 1
5 5   B   5   5   B 5 B 5   B   5   5   5   5   5   B B B B   B   B   5   5   B B B B B B B

Playing Minor Scale Songs

Although it's really outside the scope of this book, some of you may wish to experiment with the Minor Scale discussed in the music theory chapter. However, without using the technique known as 'Bending' notes (that's for later on), you will have to use the high end of your Harp to produce a Minor Scale.

This means that:
A) Your Minor Scale will be a bit piercing, and
B) Care must be taken to obtain single notes
C) some of the higher single notes may be difficult to obtain without lots of practice.

Minor Scale:

6 7 7 8 8 9 9 10
5 5 B 5 B 5 B 5

Try the haunting melody of **Greensleeves** (slightly modified):

A las my love you do me wrong   To cast me out dis courteously
6 7 8 8 9 8 8 7 6 6   7 7 6 66 6 7 6 5
S B S B S B S S B S S B S SB S S B B

for I have loved you with all my heart and who but my la ay dy Green sleeves
6 7 8 8 9 8 8 7 6 6 7 7 7 6 6 5 6 6 6
S B S B S B S S B S S B S S B B B S S

Partially Notated Songs

If you like any of these songs, try to finish them yourselves. Use trial and error to find the missing notes, and write them down in Harptab™ as you locate them.

Bob Dylan's **"Blowin' In the Wind"**:

How many roads must a man walk down
6 66 6 6 5 6 5 4 4
B BB S B S B B S B

Dylan's **"Mr. Tambourine Man"**:

Hey Mister Tambourine Man   Play a Song for me

7	7	7	6	6	6	5	5	6	6	5	4
B	B	S	S	B	B	S	B	S	B	B	B

"You Are My Sunshine":

You are my sunshine, my only sunshine, you make me happy when skies are grey

3	4	4	5	5	5	4	5	4	4 ·	4	4	5	5	6	6	6	5	5
B	B	S	B	B	B	S	B	B	B	B	S	B	S	S	S	B	S	B

"On Top of Old Smoky":

On top of old Smo-ky all covered with snow I lost my true lover a courtin' too slow

4	4	5	6	7	6	6	5	6	6	6	4	4	5	6	6	4	5	5	5	4	4
B	B	B	B	B	S	S	S	B	S	B	B	B	B	B	B	S	B	S	B	S	B

"Summertime": This song is based on the Minor Scale and all the notes are located between holes number five and eight.

Summertime an de liv in' is ea sy

8	7	8	8	7	8	8	7	6	5
B	B	B	S	B	S	B	B	S	B

Here's a section of song similar to one used in the Rolling Stone's **"Miss You":** (which itself is derived from a traditional English song called "Lovely Joan"). It is also based on a Minor Scale.

$$\dot{6}\;\dot{6}\;8\;7\;\dot{6}\;\dot{6}\;\dot{6}\;.\;\;\dot{6}\;\dot{6}\;8\;7\;\dot{6}\;\dot{6}\;\dot{6}\;.\;\;\dot{6}\;\dot{6}\;7\;\dot{6}\;....\;\;\dot{6}\;\dot{6}\;7\;\dot{6}\;....$$
$$B\;S\;S\;B\;S\;B\;S\;\;\;\;B\;S\;S\;B\;S\;B\;S\;\;\;\;B\;S\;B\;S\;\;\;\;\;\;B\;S\;B\;S$$

The Beatle's **"Give Peace A Chance.":**

All	we	are	say	ing	is	give	peace	a	chance

$$\dot{5}\;\;\dot{4}\;\;4\;\;\dot{4}\;\;\dot{3}\;.\overset{\frown}{3}\;\;\dot{5}\;\;\;\dot{5}\;\;4\;\;\overset{....}{4}\;.$$
$$B\;\;\;S\;\;\;B\;\;\;S\;\;\;B\;\;\;B\;\;S\;\;\;\;B\;\;\;S\;\;\;B$$

Playing these songs will help familiarize you with the Harp, and also with my own notation system. **But don't linger here (unless you prefer these songs to the Blues), at least listen to Sections II and III right away!**

PROLONGING HARMONICA LIFE

DON'T BLOW FOOD THROUGH IT-RINSE MOUTH AFTER EATING!
KEEP IT IN CASE WHEN NOT PLAYING!
DON'T BLOW IT TOO HARD-IT SHORTENS LIFE (HARP'S LIFE, NOT YOURS).

Section II: Playing the Blues!

Important thought to remember: A Blues structure is a 'framework' composed of 3 chords. Once we have learned this 'skeleton' structure, we will 'flesh it out' by using our own choice of notes (which will be picked largely from the Blues Scale).

Where the Blues Began:

I'm not gonna try to describe the Blues to you. If you're human, you've felt'em already. Because the type of music we call the Blues expresses feelings-and everybody has feelings.

There are Optimistic Blues and Pessimistic Blues. Self-Congratulatory Blues and Self-Destructive Blues. The Lonely Blues, the Poor Blues, the Metaphysical Blues, the Cadillac-Won't-Start Blues. Different events have different effects on different people. One person's stubbed toe is another's major catastrophe-and vice versa. But everyone has feelings-strong feelings-and thus both the right and reason to play the Blues.

What I want to do now is to give you enough historical and structural knowledge of the Blues to let you play your own-so let's jump over to Europe and Africa a thousand years ago. . .

Now, ever since emerging from the Dark Ages, the Mainstream European Musical Tradition had one major priority. That was to be able to exactly notate and reproduce any specific piece of music, with no room for deviation or personal interpretation. Thus Standard Notation and the Piano were developed. The Major and Minor Scales were used almost exclusively.

On the other continent, the Africans had a sophisticated musical tradition, but not much technology, and no written notation system. Their music was more personal and interpretive, and often improvised. Favorite songs were passed on by mouth, and changed over time. The rhythms and beats were more important, and more rigidly adhered to than an exactly repeated use of scale notes. A scale similar to the modern Blues Scale was probably used, but with enough flexibility to change or leave notes out, as each singer desired.

When the Africans were kidnapped over the 'New World' (new to Europe, that is) their music was one of the few traditions that they were able to keep.

And so the unwritten, spontaneous, personalized African musical tradition merged, mingled, and miscegenated with the highly structured, rigid, 'notated' European musical tradition: and gave Birth To The Blues!

So somewhere, somehow, in the region where the Mississippi River runs into the Gulf of Mexico-a new musical structure emerged. No one now alive knows exactly when (no tape decks back then) but this structure was so striking and expressive that it quickly spread from hamlet to hamlet, town to town, and city to city. It is now the most widespread musical structure that the world has ever known!

We'll begin our study of the Blues from a rather European and Structural point of view. Then we will gradually integrate the Bluesy and Improvisational African aspects.

Now we'll learn how to understand the most commonly played type of Blues: **The Twelve Bar Blues Structure.** And soon we'll be playing some Blues on our Harps!

"puttin' that cotton in a 'leven foot sack — 12 gauge shotgun at my back" —Traditional

1:40

The 12 Bar Blues Structure

As we no doubt remember, Chords are groups of notes that sound well when played simultaneously. **Our Blues Structure is constructed of 3 different chords that are 'stacked' together in a particular order.** Each of these 3 chords has a name (you might consider it a 'generic' name). Please **memorize** these three chord names, and don't worry about what they mean (they are very old names, and their meanings are lost in antiquity).

Tonic Chord   Subdominant Chord   Dominant Chord

Another important word to memorize is 'Bar'. One Bar equals Four Beats. They could be fast beats, slow beats, or medium beats.

Look at the Blues Structure Chart while you listen to me describe a 12 Bar Blues in words, and to Steve's musical demonstration of two 12 Bar Blues verses. Notice how the second verse starts right after the first one ends, and how both have exactly the same structure as shown on the chart. Tap your foot!

Hear how the **'Turnaround',** which is a few beats of Dominant note or Chord thrown in towards the end of the Third Tonic Phrase's 8 beats, 'announces' the end of each verse.

You've probably heard this exact structure thousands of times, in Blues, Rock, and Jazz music. Why is it so popular? Why does this particular musical framework seem to 'grab' people on a 'gut level?' I can't answer those questions - but since I first heard the Blues I've been a believer!

1:47

Two Main Types of Blues 'Introductions'

Like a book, a Blues song often begins with an introduction before the first actual verse is played. There are two common types of Blues 'Intros'.

The sixteen beat, or four bar, introduction is composed of four beats of Dominant, then four beats of Subdominant, then eight beats of Tonic with a Turnaround. Then the first verse of the song begins. In other words, a 'four bar intro' is just like the last one-third of a regular 12 Bar Blues (look at your 12 Bar Blues chart) that has been placed at the beginning of a Blues song.

The eight beat or 'two bar intro' consists of eight beats of Tonic including a Turnaround. It's exactly like the Third Tonic Phrase of a 12 Bar Blues that has been 'tacked on' to the beginning of a Blues song.

In both of these demonstrations (especially the second) Steve is making more complex use of single notes in his guitar work, as well as chords. Make sure that you recognize the underlying 12 Bar Blues Structure (look at the chart if necessary , and tap your foot) even though these last two verses are somewhat less 'structurally obvious' then the earlier demonstrations.

Spend a bit of time here. Relax, close your eyes, turn the volume up, tap your foot and let these 12 Bar blues 'changes' sink into your soul. . .

Section of Blues	Bars	Beats
First Tonic Phase	4	16
First Subdominant Phase	2	8
Second Tonic Phase	2	8
Dominant Phase	1	4
Second Subdominant Phase	1	4
Third Tonic Phase (includes turnaround)	2	8
Total	12	48

Section III: Harpin' the Blues!

Mr. Hohner made his Harp with the intention of playing Major Scale based German Folk and Classical music. For this reason, he made his instrument so that an 'F' Harmonica would easily play an 'F' Major Scale type of music. But the Afro-American folk who obtained the Harmonica after or during the 'Civil' War came from a very different musical tradition than Mr. Hohner. And they found that in order to play music that satisfied them; they had to play a very different type of scale: the **Blues Scale.** This type of scale turned out to be most easily playable when an 'F' Harmonica was used to produce a 'C' **Blues Scale.** This is sometimes called **Cross** or **Second Position Harmonica.** There are other ways to play, but for now we'll be playing only one 'key' (Blues in 'C') with our Harp. Check out my 'Cross Harp Chart' in the discography section if you wish to play other key Blues using other key Harps. Sound at all confusing? If you're using an 'F' Harp with this package - you never have to think about key at all, so don't worry!

Your Blues Chords

Here are the chords and turnaround note that we'll be using in our first Harp Blues. **Please don't worry about single notes much here,** even though I will begin to write my notation **as though** you could get the single notes. Concentrate on structure and beat, and you'll sound fine with chords.

Tonic Chord	Subdominant Chord	Dominant Chord	Turnaround Note
$\frac{123}{S}$	$\frac{345}{B}$	$\frac{345}{S}$	$\frac{1}{S}$

Pre-Blues Practice

Practice the two suck to four blow jump. Try to change after exactly four beats of each:

one two three four 2 4 2 4 2 4
                   S B S B S B

Trouble with the Low Sucks?

Each key Harp seems to have a different 'problem' note for some people, and the toughest single note to get on our 'F' Harp may be the one suck. Keep your **nose open** when you practice your one suck. Play it **softly,** and keep your nose **so open** that 90% of the air comes through your nose, and only 10% through your mouth and Harp! **Also keep your tongue as relaxed as possible.** If your one suck perversely persists in sounding 'funky', just continue on through my book and tape to Section VI, "Tone and Single Notes". Or jump up there right now for a bit of help with that one suck.

Turnaround Practice

This is the hardest part of the 12 Bar, so practice your turnaround until it feels relatively natural, and you'll be ready to Blow your first verse!

2 1 1 Breathe 2 1 1 . 2 1 1 .
S S S   S S S   S S S

Our First Harp Blues

We've practiced the hard parts, and we're primed and ready to Blow. Listen to my two 12 Bar Blues Harp verses with 'instructional vocals' for a while then play along! Use chords (like my first verse does) or single notes if you prefer (as my second verse does). Don't worry about 'tahing' until you've played this part a few times without 'tahs'.

Here's how you can avoid the 'usual' mistakes: Try to avoid confusing the Blow and the Suck sections. Make sure that your foot maintains a solid steady beat throughout (practice the footwork without Harp if necessary). Change each chord on exactly the right beat (listen carefully to my vocal instructions, and use the beats of silence to locate the next note or chord that you need). Breathe as needed during the silent beats, but keep the Harp securely pushed into your upper lip, drop your jaw and lower lip, and inhale or exhale under the Harp, not through it. This is the easiest way to catch a breath between notes without making unwanted sound or getting your Harp out of proper playing position.

"Introduction: Get ready for your ⅔ note or chord"

```
2̇ 2̇ 2̇ . 2̇ 2̇ 2̇ .        2̇ 2̇ 2̇ . 2̇ 2̇ 2̇ .        4̇ 4̇ 4̇ . 4̇ 4̇ 4̇ .
S S S   S S S  Breathe  S S S   S S S  Change   B B B   B B B
        1ˢᵗ Tonic                            to
                                                     1ˢᵗ Subdominant
```

```
2̇ 2̇ 2̇ . 2̇ 2̇ 2̇  Breathe  4̇ 4̇ 4̇ . 4̇ 4̇ 4̇ .  2̇ 2̇ 2̇  Breathe  2̇ 1 1 .
S S S   S S S          S S S   B B B    S S S           S S S
2ⁿᵈ Tonic              Dominant  2ⁿᵈ Subdom.  3ʳᵈ Tonic      Turnaround
```

50

Section IV: Trains and the Boogie!

Not all Blues songs use the 12 Bar Structure. A **Boogie** is a type of Blues that uses only the Tonic Chord in its basic structure (no Subdominants or Dominants). Let's learn a **'Train-style'** boogie that is easy, satisfying, and good for our rhythm and articulation skills. But before we can play our train, we'll have to study the difference between a Classical musician's and a Blues musician's sense of timing. Practice your 'Tuka' for a moment, while tapping your foot.

Classical Musician Timing

Down Up   Down Up   Down Up   Down Up

one and   two and   three and   four and

Blues Musician Timing: Emphasize and hold the Downbeat!

Down Up Down Up Down Up Down

one an' two an' three an' four

Down Up Down Up Down Up Down

Tuka Tuka Tuka Tah

Practice these exercises with mouth and foot (especially if you tend towards 'Hoof n' Mouth').

Simple Train

These chords represent the 'clacking' of the wheels. Play them without articulations. Satisfy all your breathing needs through the Harmonica (feel too empty?: Emphasize the Sucks! Feel too full? Blow Harder!). Lightheaded? It'll pass with a few days of practice as your respiratory system strenthens. So sit down and keep on playin'!

one two three four $\frac{\dot{1}\dot{2}\dot{3}}{S}$ $\frac{\dot{1}\dot{2}\dot{3}}{S}$ $\frac{\dot{1}\dot{2}\dot{3}}{B}$ $\frac{\dot{1}\dot{2}\dot{3}}{B}$ $\frac{\dot{1}\dot{2}\dot{3}}{S}$ $\frac{\dot{1}\dot{2}\dot{3}}{S}$ $\frac{\dot{1}\dot{2}\dot{3}}{B}$ $\frac{\dot{1}\dot{2}\dot{3}}{B}$ $\frac{\dot{1}\dot{2}\dot{3}}{S}$ $\frac{\dot{1}\dot{2}\dot{3}}{S}$ $\frac{\dot{1}\dot{2}\dot{3}}{B}$ $\frac{\dot{1}\dot{2}\dot{3}}{B}$ etc.

Adding some articulations will help your train to sound 'trainier'. I'm calling out **Sucka** and **Blowa** on the tape, but you can say **Tuka** or **Chukka** or **Chugga** or **Dada** on each beat (whichever sounds best or easiest for you). Do the Suck articulations still make you 'tongue-tied?' Then start out by only articulating the Blow chords. **And remember to swing that rhythm! Emphasize those downbeats!**

one two three four
Suck $\frac{123}{S}$ Suck $\frac{123}{S}$ Blowa $\frac{123}{B}$ Blowa $\frac{123}{B}$ Dada $\frac{\dot{1}\dot{2}\dot{3}}{S}$ Dada $\frac{\dot{1}\dot{2}\dot{3}}{S}$ Dada $\frac{\dot{1}\dot{2}\dot{3}}{B}$ Dada $\frac{\dot{1}\dot{2}\dot{3}}{B}$ etc.

What does our train need now? **A whistle!** Make sure that you always **Suck** the whistle, and **exhale lots** on that beat of silence after the second part of the whistle. Then you'll be ready for the Suck chords of the train again. Add a hand wah-wah to the whistle if you like.

$\frac{\dot{4}\dot{\dot{5}}}{5}$ exhale $\frac{\dot{4}\dot{\dot{5}}}{5}$ exhale one two three four

Sucka Sucka Blowa Blowa Sucka Sucka Blowa Blowa get ready for the whistle

$\frac{123}{S}$ $\frac{123}{S}$ $\frac{123}{B}$ $\frac{123}{B}$ $\frac{123}{S}$ $\frac{123}{S}$ $\frac{123}{B}$ $\frac{123}{B}$ $\frac{123}{S}$ $\frac{123}{S}$ $\frac{123}{B}$ $\frac{123}{B}$

Suuck exhale $\frac{45}{S}$ Suuck exhale $\frac{45}{S}$ Sucka $\frac{123}{S}$ Sucka $\frac{123}{S}$ Blowa $\frac{123}{B}$ Blowa $\frac{123}{B}$ and so on ...

Play the train while you walk (or run-if it's an express train). Let each footfall represent one beat - it's actually easier to play and walk than it is to play while tapping. **And think about that train!** Make it real - because playing the harmonica is not merely an oral or intellectual exercise. Harpin' is a way of expressing real ideas and emotions.

Is it coming towards you (getting louder) or going away (softer)? Leaving you at the station (the beat speeds up, and the volume drops) or approaching you (volume increases, speed decreases until train stops)?

Q: What would the train sound like if you were lying under the trestle drinking Sterno when it came on through?

A: The speed of the train would stay constant and fairly fast, but it would start very softly, and increase in volume until it was intolerably loud, then fade out completely. Sterno drinkers tend to be a sad lot, so the whistle would probably need a heavy moaning hand wah-wah effect.

Section V: More Rhythm in our 12 Bars

We can make our 12 Bar Blues more interesting by adding some 'rhythm' to our chords. That is, we will break some or all of the beats into smaller time units, instead of just playing the chord once per beat as we did before. Here are three simple rhythm patterns to use with your Blues chords:

Rhythm Pattern #1: Cut the 'tah' off very sharply, so that there are actually 1½ beats of silence in each bar (4 beats), instead of just one. I'll use an exclamation mark to indicate the sharp cut-off. Practice saying the pattern verbally, then articulate it through your four blow and two suck chords. Once you've gotten the hang of that, 'tuka' your way through an entire 12 Bar! The turnaround may take some practice.

one two three four Tuka Tuka Tah! · Tuka Tuka Tah! ·

Rhythm Pattern #2: Once again - cut that last 'tah' off sharply. Practice it with your chords, then run it through a 12 Bar. I use a short turnaround in my example (just one beat of one suck on the 'tah' part of the last rhythm pattern of the verse).

Tuketa Tuketa Tah! · Tuketa Tuketa Tah! ·

Rhythm Pattern #3: This one is my favorite of the three. Don't cut the 'tahs' off too sharply. Practice it, and then 12 Bar it. It provides the best turnaround of these patterns (illustrated below).

Tah Tuketa Tah ·

Tah	Tu ke ta Tah	Tah	Tu ke ta Tah
2	I I I I ·	2	I I I I ·
S	S S S S	S	S S S S

54

Now is a good time to go the practice 12 Bars at the end of Side Two of this tape. Turn the lights down, the volume up, and wail these rhythm articulations on your Tonic, Subdominant, and Dominant chords. You might even feel adventurous, and make up some rhythm articulations of your own! Flap that tongue.

Section VI: Tone and Single Notes

1:65

If you've been avoiding single notes so far, now just might be a good time to begin thinking about starting to attempt the process of obtaining a clear single note. Listen to my demonstration on tape, and learn to listen to yourself, too. Soon you'll be able to hear quite clearly whether you're getting one hole or two. Review the single note text in Section I if you need to. **Keep trying, but don't get discouraged about single notes: you can play plenty using chords!**

For purest tone, keep your throat open, almost as though you were yawning. **Let your tongue lay relaxed** in the bottom of your mouth, like a sea cucumber lying on the bottom of the ocean. No muscle! **Avoid neck or shoulder tenseness** also. Relax and 'think' that tone in or out of the Harp. For a pleasant musical/respiratory 'meditation', take your favorite hole and inhale then exhale as **slowly** and **relaxedly** as you can for a few moments. **Stretch** each in and out sound for as long as you can hold them. If you're the competitive type, time yourself on this exercise today, and then in a month. You'll be surprised and pleased!

A 'Funky' One

Does your one suck persist in sounding 'funky?' You're just jumping the gun on the technique we call **'Bending'!** Here I demonstrate three full bends on one suck, and one slide from normal to bent tone. Sounds like "doo-doo-doo-dahoooh." We'll learn more about bends on the other side of the cassette, and much of Volume II will be devoted to the mastery of the bending technique. And don't worry too much about your 'funky' one suck - just review my 'Trouble With the Low Sucks' section and 'bend' away if you have to. Most of our current songs will work better with an unbent one suck however.

1:69

A New Chord Rhythm

We'll turn this exciting John Mayall-style rhythm pattern into a complete 12 Bar on Side Two. Get the timing down now, and push that air!

.... $\overline{123}$ $\overline{123}$ $\overline{123}$ $\overline{123}$ $\overline{123}$ $\overline{123}$ $\overline{123}$ $\overline{123}$ $\overline{123}$ $\overline{123}$ ..
　　 S　 S　 B　 S　 S　 B　 S　 S　 B　 S

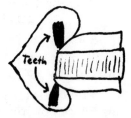

 ## One Last Side One Hint

Spend a few minutes each day picturing yourself playing well and enjoying it. This is especially important if you're prone to self-criticism and impatience with yourself. On Side Two we'll use some relaxation, visualization, and subliminal suggestion techniques to allow you to put some 'soul' into your playing!

 1:71

End of Tape Cassette Side One

Section VII: Some New Holes to Use

2:00

Do you remember my discussion of 'octave' notes in the Music Theory chapter of this book? Octave notes are notes that sound almost exactly like each other, although they may vary in highness or lowness. All octave notes use the same 'letter name'.

Please look at the picture of 'your F Harp' in Section I. Notice the four 'C' notes, four 'F' notes and three 'G' notes. These octave notes can be used interchangeably in our 12 Bars, as long as you can at least come close to hitting them singly. We call these notes the:

Basic Tonic Notes (C): **Basic Subdominant Notes (F):** **Basic Dominant Notes (G):**

$$\frac{2}{S} \quad \frac{3}{B} \quad \frac{6}{B} \quad \frac{9}{B} \qquad \frac{1}{B} \quad \frac{4}{B} \quad \frac{7}{B} \quad \frac{10}{B} \qquad \frac{1}{S} \quad \frac{4}{S} \quad \frac{8}{S}$$

Be careful with the high notes on your F Harp. Try using the above High Substitute notes, but play'em **gently.** Too much air can injure the tiny metal reeds.

Here's a new 12 Bar for you. Notice how I use various **Tah, Tada,** and **Tadada** articulations, and also longer held notes. Get rid of lots of air on the four beats of one blow, so that you can play the 5 beats of two suck and two beats of four suck (turnaround).

[musical notation with numbers and S/B markings]

Tonic   Subdom.   Tonic   Dom. Sub Tonic Turnaround

Experiment with these 'interchangeable' Tonic, Subdominant, and Dominant notes during the Tonic, Subdominant, and Dominant phrases of our practice 12 Bars.

Information Flowing Faster? You're In Charge of the Buttons of Your Tape Deck! Work at Your Own Pace!

2:05

Section VIII: The New Train Boogie

Our new train combines chords with the single note one suck. You may want to angle the entire high end of the Harp away from your mouth to obtain an easier single one suck (a bit of two suck in there won't kill you). Start it off slowly, and without articulations. Remember to adjust the force of your inhaling and exhaling to keep a comfortable amount of air in your lungs at all times.

$$\underset{S}{123} \quad \underset{B}{123} \quad \underset{S}{1} \quad \underset{B}{123} \qquad \underset{S}{123} \quad \underset{B}{123} \quad \underset{S}{1} \quad \underset{B}{123} \quad etc.$$

(Angle) (harp) (away) — (harp)

Add some **'chugga'** or **'chukka'** articulations for a 'trainier' sound.

Sucka Blowa Suka Blowa — Dada Dada Dada Dada

$$\underset{S}{123} \quad \underset{B}{123} \quad \underset{S}{1} \quad \underset{B}{123} \qquad \underset{S}{123} \quad \underset{B}{123} \quad \underset{S}{1} \quad \underset{B}{123} \quad etc.$$

This 'cut-off' train pattern will be of use later. When we start adding some 'refinements' to our train, that extra beat of silence will come in handy.

Sucka Blowa Suka Blowa Sucka Blow Suck

$$\underset{S}{123} \quad \underset{B}{123} \quad \underset{S}{1} \quad \underset{B}{123} \quad \underset{S}{123} \quad \underset{B}{123} \quad \underset{S}{123} \quad .$$

58

Section IX: The Blues Scale

This is the 'musical alphabet' of Blues Music. And soon we can begin using the Blues Scale to 'flesh out' our Blues Structure, instead of just playing the structure by itself as we have been. Listen to how **right** it sounds when I play the Blues Scale against Steve's Blues Structure background. Did you like my demonstration of the Blues Scale on **Tin-Flute**? Then see my sales pitch on the back page!

How to Play the Blues Scale

Somewhere in the Deep South, perhaps as many as a hundred years ago, an unknown Afro-American musician decided to play some Blues style music on the Harmonica. But the Major Scale built into the instrument (from four blow to seven blow) by Mr. Hohner just didn't sound very Bluesy, so our anonymous musical forefather (or foremother, as the case may be) found an alternate way to produce a Bluesier Scale. This new Harmonica Blues Scale could be played most easily from two suck to six blow, with 'bends' required on the three and four suck notes.

We need to bend notes to produce a **complete** Blues Scale, but don't worry much about bending yet (unless you'd like to worry about your as yet unwanted one suck bend). It is one of the most important Blues Harp techniques, but I found in my classes that it is discouraging and not useful to try to teach it too soon. So, listen again to my four suck bend and two suck bend after a month, and then grab yourself a Volume Two. Bending will be heavily emphasized there, how to do it, and when. I have tons of info on bending: you may learn more than you want to know!

My notation system uses a little "b" to indicate a bend. So the most accessible Blues Scale looks like this:

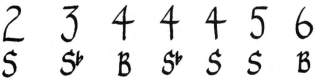

Fortunately for us, most of the Blues Scale notes do not require bending. Since we know that any combination of Blues Scale notes **must** sound Bluesy, let's choose a few of these non-bent Blues Scale notes and make up some Blues 'Licks'. **'Licks' are small combinations of notes that we like and memorize.**

High End Blues Scale Notes

Locate your six blow. Use the 'tongue-hole-counting' method or the 'forefinger-to-lip' method described on page 31 if you need to. The more you use six blow, the easier it will become to find. Can you hit it singly? If not, these licks won't be too much fun to play, and you may want to skip this section until you've mastered single noting. . .

These licks fit just fine into a 12 Bar. Let's get a few nice ones together.

Tah Tah Tah   Too Chordy

6 5 4 . 6 5 4 . 6 5 4 . 7 6 5   6 5 4   5 4 3 .
B S S   B S S   B S S   B   S   S

Now let's add some articulation. Use Dada or Tata if you like. We'll be using these new licks along with Steve's 12 Bar backing soon.

6 6 5 5 4 . 6 6 5 5 4 . 6 6 5 5 4 . 6 6 5 5 4 .
B B S S S   B B S S S   B B S S S   B B S S S

Here's a two beat Blues Scale Lick. If saying a "Blow-Suck" Tuka or Dada's difficult, just remember to play six blow on the down beat and five suck on the upbeat without any tongue articulations. Just use the articulations written above the notes to give yourself an idea of how the timing should sound.

$$
\overset{\text{Tuka Tah}}{6\,5\,4} \quad 6\,5\,4 \quad 6\,5\,4 \quad \overset{\text{Tuka Tah}}{6\,5\,4}
$$
$$
B\,S\,S \quad B\,S\,S \quad B\,S\,S \quad B\,S\,S \qquad :
$$

Now add another beat of four suck
and a beat of silence.

$$
\overset{\text{Tuka Tah Tah}}{6\,5\,4\,4} \;.\; \overset{\text{Tuka Tah Tah}}{6\,5\,4\,4} \;.\; \text{etc.}
$$
$$
B\,S\,S\,S \qquad B\,S\,S\,S
$$

Practice your four suck to six blow jump. Now combine two 'two-beaters' and one 'four-beater' to get:

$$
6\,5\,4 \quad 6\,5\,4 \quad 6\,5\,4\,4 \;.\; 6\,5\,4 \quad 6\,5\,4 \quad 6\,5\,4\,4 \;.
$$
$$
B\,S\,S \quad B\,S\,S \quad B\,S\,S\,S \qquad B\,S\,S \quad B\,S\,S \quad B\,S\,S\,S
$$

Play this 8 beat lick throughout a 12 Bar. Sure sounds right, doesn't it? Vary your volume for interest. Any of these licks will sound good and Bluesy when played against a Blues Structure backing, even though they wouldn't create or indicate the Blues Structure if played by themselves.
Changing the timing of the above lick slightly provides us with a new lick. Try a Tah Tuka type pattern:

$$
\overset{\text{Tah Tuka}}{6\,5\,4} \quad \overset{\text{Tah Tuka}}{6\,5\,4} \quad \overset{\text{Tah Tuka}}{6\,5\,4}
$$
$$
B\,S\,S \quad B\,S\,S \quad B\,S\,S
$$

Add a beat of six blow and a beat of silence:

6 5 4 6 . 6 5 4 6 .
B S S B   B S S B

Once again, two plus two plus four equals eight beats and we can plug our new lick into a 12 Bar:

654 654 6546 . 654 654 6546 .
B S S B S S B S S B   B S S B S S B S S B

Since 'licks alone do not a 12 Bar make,' we can delineate the Blues Structure with our trusty two suck, four blow, four suck chord pattern from Section III, and throw some bars of licks in to liven up a solo performance. This allows us to use licks in a 12 Bar format even if we don't have a guitarist on tap! Can you create some similar chord/lick verses of your own?

Here's a new Tah Tuketa Tah lick:

$$\overset{\bullet\bullet}{6\,5\,4\,5\,6} \;.\; \overset{Tah\;Tuketa\;Tah}{\overset{\bullet\bullet}{6\,5\,4\,5\,6}}.$$

$$B\;S\;S\;S\;B \qquad\qquad B\;S\;S\;S\;B$$

Try it in a chord pattern and lick 12 Bar. Notice my simplified chord notation. The extra four suck instead of six blow on the last lick creates a clearer turnaround - and now go burn up those practice 12 Bars at the end of this cassette.

one two three four $\underline{123}$. 65456 , $\underline{123}$. 65456 . $\underline{345}$. 65456 .
                          Tonic S   B S S S B   S   B S S S B Sub. B   B S S S B

Tonic $\underline{123}$. 65456 . $\underline{345}$. $\underline{345}$. $\underline{123}$. 65454 .
       S   B S S S B Dom. S   Subdom. B   Tonic S   B S S S

2:30

Section X: Bluesifying Our Boogie!

Are you practiced up on the train from the end of Section VIII? If not, go back and get down.
The notation for our new **"Shake Whistle"** looks like this: ⌇⌒
So the complete whistle is notated as follows, and you can shake either your hands or your head - whichever is easier.

$$\overset{\overset{\bullet\bullet\bullet}{\bullet\bullet\bullet}}{\underset{\underset{S}{\sim}}{4\!\!5}} \cdot \overset{\overset{\bullet\bullet\bullet}{\bullet\bullet\bullet}}{\underset{\underset{S}{\sim}}{4\!\!5}} \cdot \overset{\overset{\bullet\bullet\bullet}{\bullet\bullet\bullet}}{\underset{\underset{S}{\sim}}{4\!\!5}} \cdot \overset{\overset{\bullet\bullet\bullet}{\bullet\bullet\bullet}}{\underset{\underset{S}{\sim}}{4\!\!5}} \cdot$$

The **'oy-oy-oy' whistle (or 'Jewish' whistle - remember that I did shorten my name from Harpowitz) is a 'pre-bending' effect.** Say **'oyyyy',** with a long, drawn-out 'y'part. Your tongue should end upflattened and almost clamped between your back molars. Then open your mouth back up for the 'O' part of the 'Oy'. The entire phrase perhaps should be written **'Oy-yoy-yoy!'.** Exaggerate the movement of the tongue as much as possible for maximum sound change. Use both of these new whistles with either of your trains.

$$\overset{\overset{oy\ yoy\ yoy}{\bullet\ \bullet\ \bullet}}{\underset{\underset{S}{}}{4\ 5}} \cdot \overset{\overset{oy\ yoy\ yoy}{\bullet\ \bullet\ \bullet}}{\underset{\underset{S}{}}{4\ 5}} \cdot \overset{\overset{oy\ yoy\ yoy}{\bullet\ \bullet\ \bullet}}{\underset{\underset{S}{}}{4\ 5}} \cdot$$

Now we'll learn to use a six blow, five suck, and four suck lick as a whistle following our "cut-off" train pattern from Section VIII. This gives us one beat of silence to search out the six blow after leaving the train chord pattern.

Play it just like I do, or use it as a boogie backing, and throw in your own licks along with it.

64

If you're learning to play with a friend, have him or her provide a nice, solid wheel-clackin' train that you can improvise various whistles and licks to. Remember-tap your foot! All aboooooard!

one two three four

Sucka Blowa Sucka Blowa

123 123 T 123   123 123 T 123   123 123 T 123
 S   B S B   S   B S B   S   B S B

get ready for the whistle   shake   whistle

123 123 T 123   45 • 45 •   123 123 T 123
 S   B S B   Breathe Breathe   S   B S B
                  S   S

oy yoy yoy oy yoy yoy   cut off pattern   get ready for lick

123 123 T 123   45 • 45 • 123 123 T 123 123 123 123 •
 S   B S B   Breathe Breathe S   B S B   S   B   S

                          cut off pattern

654 654 6546 • 123 123 T 123 123 123 123 • 654 • 654 •
B S B S BSSB   S   B S B   S   B   S   BSS   BSS

          cut off pattern   Sucka Blowa Sucka Blowa

123 123 T 123 123 123 123 • 6 5 4 • 123 123 T 123 for a while
 S   B S B   S   B   S   B S S   S   B S S

65

2:36

Section XI: Some Famous Licks

We're going to learn one of the best-loved Blues licks ever! It provides a great Tonic Framework on which we can build all kinds of other licks, and is also well suited for singing along with.

The timing of this low-end Blues Scale lick is quite sophisticated, so if you're not familiar with the "I'm a (Wo) Man" type lick already, you'd better listen to it lots before trying to Blow it. Practice saying this 4 beat rhythm pattern which contains 2 beats of silence. Get ready to say that first 'tah' as your foot lifts right after tapping down on the "three" of the countdown.

Down   Down   Down   Up
one   two   three   Tah   Tuka   Tah .. Tah   Tuka   Tah .. Tah

Now practice your two suck to four blow jump for a moment. Try to jump accurately to center on four blow, even if you can't single note it. Chords work well enough for this lick, as long as your timing (and your grasp of the proper Suck or Blow pattern) is right.

one two three   2432 . 2432 . 2432 ..
                 S B S S   S B S S   S B S S

Practice this lick lots! Try to feel **exactly** where all four downbeats (dots) fall, and emphasize them. People often sing during the 2 beat 'Breaks' while playing this one (usually every other line rhymes). A great number of well-known Blues songs use this as their main lick. There are also many traditional licks that can be 'sandwiched' into the breaks. Here's an easy one:

one two three 1̲2̲3̲ 1̲2̲3̲ 1̲2̲3̲ 1̲2̲3̲ . . 1̲2̲3̲ 1̲2̲3̲ 1̲2̲3̲ 1̲2̲3̲ . .
                   S   S   B   S   S   S   B   S

Can you hear and see how the downbeats and upbeats of this above 'sandwich' lick are exactly the same as those of the "I'm a (Wo) Man) lick? All of our 'sandwiching' licks will have to begin on upbeats so get used to that timing right now.

Feeling pretty slick? Then practice your two suck to six blow jump so that we can sandwich a six blow, five suck, four suck lick into our new lick's silent beats.

6̲6̲5̲6̲ . .   6̲6̲5̲4̲ . .   6̲6̲5̲4̲6̲ . .   6̲6̲5̲4̲6̲ . .

Try perhaps a: B B S B   or a: B B S S   or: B B S S B   B B S S B

Any two beat lick with similar timing will fit in well. Or you can fit two beats of singing in! **Anyone can sing ('specially if no one is listening).** So learn to play, or play along with, or sing along with my

"I'm A Man" type Boogie here. As far as breathing goes; either breathe during the silences or through your Harp; there are enough Sucks and Blows both so that your supply of oxygen should feel challenged but not threatened.

```
... 2432 .. 2432 .. 2432 .. 2432 .. 2432  •   •   2432  •  •  2432
    SBSS    SBSS    SBSS    SBSS    SBSS  I play my harp SBSS to get this lick SBSS

in order to sing 2432 you gotta be quick 2432   123 123 123 123  2432
                 SBSS                     SBSS   S   S   B   S    SBSS

123 123 123 123 2432  123 123 123 123 2432  123 123 123 123
 S   S   B   S  SBSS   S   S   B   S  SBSS   S   S   B   S

2 4 3 2 6 6 5 4 2 4 3 2 6 6 5 4 2 4 3 2 6 6 5 4 6
S B S S B B S S S B S S B B S S S B S S B B S S B

2 4 3 2 6 6 5 4 6 2 4 3 2  •  • 2 4 3 2  • • 2 4 3 2
S B S S B B S S B S B S S    S B S S     S B S S    etc.
```

The Rest of This Package

In these final sections you will find a variety of improvisational techniques, and one well-known piece of 'Classical' Blues. Depending on your own strengths and weaknesses, certain techniques will be easier or harder for you. For this reason I suggest a 'shotgun approach' to the rest of my package. Try each different style or technique for a short time. Then enjoy the ones that you find easy, and practice the ones you find hard!

2:43

Section XII: The Simple Jamming Rules™

Now that you're gaining a 'feel' for the Blues, I'm going to give you three simple rules that will allow you to safely and accurately create your own improvised 12 Bars. These rules will help you to choose from those notes that 'fit in best' with either the Tonic, the Subdominant, or the Dominant Chord of your Blues Structure.

Why Do these Rules Work? Because the Tonic Jamming Rule only includes those notes that fit in perfectly with the Tonic Chord, the Subdominant Jamming Rule only includes those notes that fit the Subdominant Chord, and the Dominant Rule only includes those notes that fit in with the Dominant Chord. So we are doing something quite similar to what Steve was doing in his 8 Beat Introduction and verse back in Section II. **Instead of playing all the chord notes together as chords during each section of the 12 Bar we are playing each note separately to form improvised licks.**

The Simple Jamming Rules act like training wheels for your Blues Improvisation. That is, they allow you to immediately begin creating Blues Music of your own without the danger of hitting notes that sound wrong.

These rules are so 'safe' that they will eventually become boring or limiting if we use them for too long (ever see anyone on a cruising 10 Speed Bicycle with Training Wheels?). There are lots of wild and crazy and tense notes out there that we'll want to use in our 12 Bar soon; as soon as we can control what we already have (you guessed it — more Volume Two material).

 Tonic Jamming Rule: Use notes one suck through five suck (Low Sucks)
Subdominant Jamming Rule: Use any Blow notes
Dominant Jamming Rule: Use Middle Suck notes (4-6) or any High Sucks

Now practice identifying your Low (1-5) Suck notes, your Blow (1-10) notes, and your High (either 4-6 or 4-10) Suck notes.

Then listen carefully to my two 12 Bar verses of Simple Jamming Rule Blues and try to hear and understand what I'm doing. In the first verse I just 'randomly flail around' (using the Simple Jamming Rules for each phrase of the Blues, of course) and in verse two I use more single notes and articulations. I won't notate these verses since the idea now is to create music **yourself** with these rules, not to copy my licks.

Learning to identify the Harp notes that other people are playing will help you later on when you may want to learn to play along with, and pick up licks from records and other people. It's not too easy, though, and I must admit that it took me years to be able to listen to a Harp piece and know exactly which notes were being Blown or Sucked (and I'm still wrong, at times). But you can quickly learn (especially with repeated listenings) to tell 'more or less' what's happening (whether it's Blow or Suck, High or Low, etc.).

So play along with my two demonstration verses, and just let my vocal instructions remind you when to use your Low Suck, Blow, or Middle Suck notes. And if you should accidentally hit, say, a six suck (too high) during your Tonic (as I do in verse two, first tonic) or a three suck (too low) during the Dominant, don't be self-critical. Just don't **linger** on that 'wrong' note, and read what Jimi Hendrix had to say about such 'wrong' notes, below. **Understand these Rules? Then go to the 12 Bar Backing Section and wail!**

The Simple Jamming Rule style of improvisation may prove more interesting if you can obtain some single notes and clear articulations as illustrated in sample verse 2. It's a good motivation for some strict **Technique** practice! But, like almost all of the following Jamm styles - the Simple Jamming Rules are fun even with chords!

The Tonic Jamm Rule 'Sandwich' Boogie

We can use the Tonic Jamming Rule to create licks that fit into the two beat silences of our "I'm a (Wo) Man" lick. Just keep your ear on the rhythm of the two beat silence and use lots of slides and articulations with the Low Suck notes.

one two three 2 4 3 2 any low sucks 2 4 3 2 any low sucks 2 4 3 2 etc.
                 S B S S   S B S S   S B S S

Section XIII: Thematic Use of the Simple Jamming Rules™

Here's an easy way to create clear, cohesive, 12 Bar Blues that follow a single 'theme' throughout an entire verse. Once again, we'll use the Simple Jamming Rules, but this time in a slightly more 'organized' and less improvisational way.

Choose any four beat (one bar) note pattern (which we'll call our basic 'theme') from the notes of the Tonic Jamming Rule. Practice it, and **memorize both the rhythm of the lick and the motion of your hand as you play it.**

$$2\ 2\ 2\ 2\ 32 \bullet$$
$$S\ S\ S\ S\ S\ S$$
hole hole hole hole hole to the right original hole •

We can **'translate'** this same lick into **'Subdominant language'** by beginning the lick on four blow (or any Blow) and using the same rhythm and hand motion that we used on the Tonic theme. Likewise, we 'translate' our Tonic theme into **'Dominant language'** by using the same rhythm and hand motion on the Middle or High Suck notes.

Tonic
$$2\ 2\ 2\ 2\ 32$$
$$S\ S\ S\ S\ S\ S$$
• Subdom.
$$4\ 4\ 4\ 4\ 54$$
$$B\ B\ B\ B\ B\ B$$
, Domin.
$$4\ 4\ 4\ 4\ 54$$
$$S\ S\ S\ S\ S\ S$$
•

72

Put these Tonic, Subdominant, and Dominant Themes together in a **standard 12 Bar format** (with a Turnaround added) and you have a thematic 12 Bar Blues!

Begin with 4 Bars of Tonic Theme.
Then 2 Bars of Subdominant Theme plus 2 more Bars of Tonic Theme.
1 Bar of Dominant Theme and 1 Bar of Subdominant Theme.
End with 1 last Bar of Tonic Theme and a 1 Bar Turnaround.

Tonic   2 2 2 2 3 2 .   2 2 2 2 3 2 .   2 2 2 2 3 2 .   2 2 2 2 3 2 .
         5 5 5 5 5 5   5 5 5 5 5 5   5 5 5 5 5 5   5 5 5 5 5 5

Subd.   4 4 4 4 5 4 .   4 4 4 4 5 4 .   2 2 2 2 3 2 .   2 2 2 2 3 2 .
         B B B B B B   B B B B B B Ton 5 5 5 5 5 5   5 5 5 5 5 5

Dom.   4 4 4 4 5 4 .   Subd. 4 4 4 4 5 4 .
         5 5 5 5 5 5   B B B B B B

Tonic   2 2 2 2 3 2 .   5 slide 1 1 .
         5 5 5 5 5 5   5   5 5
                         Turnaround

73

Try creating another Thematic 12 Bar, using exactly the same process as above. Practice the rhythm and hand motion on the Tonic Theme, then 'translate' to 'Subdominant language' by Blowing and into 'Dominant language' by High Sucking.

Tonic $\dot{1}\dot{4}\overset{\frown}{3}\dot{2}$. Subdominant $\dot{1}\dot{4}\overset{\frown}{3}\dot{2}$, Dominant $\dot{4}\dot{7}\overset{\frown}{6}\dot{5}$.

S S S S   B B B B   S S S S

Getting Wild and Breaking Expectations

Play this new theme as a 12 Bar, but get wilder than you did with the 22 22 32 theme! Musical Psychologists (Krahenbuhl et al, from Yale) have found that listeners like to be surprised! So vary your theme slightly, in these ways:

1) Vary where on the Harp you play your Subdominant theme (it's the safest to 'mess around' with). Try it low for the First Subdominant and higher for the Second Subdominant. Maintain that rhythm and hand motion, though.

2) Throw in a bar's worth of the appropriate Simple Jamming Rule occasionally. The last bar of any phrase is probably the best time to do this, as illustrated, or the Second Subdominant bar.

3) Change the articulation or rhythm of the theme **slightly** from bar to bar.

4) Finally, if you're technically up to it, throw in a bar of six blow-five suck-four suck Blues Scale notes anywhere. It's got to sound good!

And don't worry too much about what you're doing because Bluespeople never make (musical) mistakes... just Surprises! Act confident and keep right on playing — and no one

will be the wiser! Jimi Hendrix said the "Blues is playing the Wrong notes in the right places!"

1 4 3 2 . 1 4 3 2 . 1 4 3 . Low Suck Jamm . 1 4 3 2 . Blow it again . 1 4 3 2 .
S S S S   S S S S   S S S   B B B B   B B B B
Tonic   Subd.

1 4 3 2 . Low Suck Jamm . 4 7 6 5 . Any Blow Jamm . 1 4 3 2 . 6 slide 1 1 .
S S S S   S S S S   S S S S   S S S S
Tonic   Dom.   Subdom   Tonic   Turnaround

1 4 3 2 . 1 4 3 2 . 1 4 3 . 6 6 5 5 4 . 1 4 3 2 . 6 5 4 .
S S S S   S S S S   S S S   B B S S S   B B B B   B S S
Tonic   Subd.

1 4 3 2 . 1 4 3 2 . 4 7 6 5 . 4 7 6 5 . 1 4 3 2 . 6 5 4 4 .
S S S S   S S S S   S S S S   B B B B   S S S S   B S S S
Tonic   Dom.   Subd.   Tonic   Turnaround

More Thematic 12 Bars

Make up some thematics of your own, and play them either solo or along with Steve's Backing 12 Bars at the end of this tape. Use the techniques described in 'Getting Wild and Breaking Expectations' to - well, get wild and break expectations! Here are a few sample Tonic Themes along with their appropriate Subdominants and Dominants.

Tonic Theme	Translate by Blowing into	Subdom. Theme	Translate by High Suck to	Domin. Theme
22 554 . SS SSS		44 776 . BB BBB	OR TRY	11 332 . BB BBB	44 776. SS SSS
545 2 . S SSS		545 2 . B BB B	OR TRY	6563 . BBB B	767 4 . SSS S
33 3342 SS SS SS		55 5564 BB BB BB	OR TRY	22 2231 BB BB BB	77 7785 SS SS SS

76

'Room to Move' or 'One Way Out' Type Thematic 12 Bar

Not all Thematic Blues are based on the Simple Jamming Rules. Our new Blues verse uses the chord rhythm pattern from the very end of Side One, and carries it throughout an entire 12 Bar Blues Structure. The timing of the original theme changes somewhat during the Dominant and Second Subdominant phrases, yet the entire verse has a charming and exciting cohesiveness.

This 12 Bar Blues is quite similar to two famous songs: **John Mayall's 'Room to Move' and Sonny Boy Williamson II's 'One Way Out'.** You might want to listen to the original versions, and hear what the 'masters' do to this simple thematic.

Practice the tonic lick of this verse (go back to the end of Side One for a moment of practice if you need to):

.... 123 123 123 123 123 123 123 123 123 123 ..
     S   S   B   S   S   B   S   S   B   S

Once you've mastered the Tonic part, listen to my description of the corresponding Subdominant lick. It has the same rhythm as the Tonic lick, but with the Blows and Sucks reversed. You can hit the three suck singly (even 'pinch' it with your lips for a Bluesy sound) or use a three and four suck chord.

45 45 34 45 45 34 45 45 34 45 ..
B   B   S   B   B   S   B   B   S   B

Since the breath reversal is a bit tricky, practice going back and forth between the Tonic and Subdominant licks. Tap your foot to maintain a continuous rhythm.

Now listen to, and practice, the Dominant and Second Subdominant segments of our new thematic.

dwah   dwah da   dwah da   dwah da

45   45 45   45 45   45 45   45 ...
S   S S   S S   S S   B

After putting all the component parts into their proper places, we'll play the entire verse slowly. Then speed up, the faster, the better!

.... 123 123 123 123 123 123 123 123 123 123 ..
Tonic S S B S S B S S B S

123 123 123 123 123 123 123 123 123 123 ..
S S B S S B S S B S

45 45 34 45 45 34 45 45 34 45 ..
Subdom B B S B B S B B S B

123 123 123 123 123 123 123 123 123 123 ..
Tonic S S B S S B S S B S

dwah dwah da dwah da dwah da

45 45 45 45 45 45 45 45 ...
Dom. S S S S S S S Subd. B

123 123 123 123 123 123 123 123 123 123 ..
Tonic S S B S S B S S B S

78

But start out playing it as slowly as you need to. Most of you will want to read the notation while you play. **This is 'Classical' music — because it has been written down for posterity — as 'Classical' as any piece by Beethoven or Brahms.** I truly feel that calling **only** music written during a certain period 'Classical' (say 1600-1850 AD) is **'Age-ist'** in the most broad sense of the word!

This is **not** improvisation, but certain pieces of Blues music work so well that we want to be able to reproduce them exactly. We will be continuing to use this song in Volume II, as there are all kinds of improvisatory 'frills' that can be added to it.

Helpful Hints:

You may someday, in a fit of inventiveness, want to 'mix and match' the various segments of different 12 Bars together. Try plugging the 'Room to Move Style' Dominant and Second Subdominant phrases into one of your other thematic Blues instead of the Dominant and Second Subdominant that you've been using. All of the various Tonic phrases are interchangeable with any other Tonics, all Subdominant phrases with any other Subdominants, and Dominant phrases with any other Dominants. Why, some of the new combinations you come up with **may** even sound good together! Experiment!

Section XIV: 'Changeless' Jamms

If we want to play 12 Bar Blues music by ourselves, it's important that we clearly indicate the Tonic, Subdominant, and Dominant chord changes. Otherwise, our music won't follow the time honored, rigidly structured 12 Bar Blues pattern.

The Simple Jamming Rules, the Thematic Blues, and memorized verses such as the one you just learned make it simple to maintain a 12 Bar format. **But sometimes we won't want to have to think about subtleties like changing from Tonic to Subdominant to Dominant chords. We'll just want to Jamm, to 'Blow from the Gut'.**

These **'Changeless Jamm'** styles will make it easier to do just that. They allow us to play along with Guitar backing using licks that fit in throughout the 12 Bar Structure. **You see, types of licks that feature mostly Tonic notes (that is, notes that fit in well during the Tonic chord) will sound good anywhere during a 12 Bar Verse.** So we let **Steve** worry about maintaining the rhythm and chord changes (he's good at it), and we merely tap our feet along with his rhythm and 'plug in' our **Tonic Based 'Lead' Harp** licks as we please! **'Lead'** Harp generally means that we are letting someone else provide the rhythm and structure. **They are providing the 'skeleton' of our 'Blues Body', and we are 'fleshing it out' with our Harps!**

Bob Dylan Style Jamming

These are the generalized type of licks that my first 'Harp-hero', Bob Dylan, used in his earlier recordings. Dylan was not technically an excellent Blues Harpist, but his guitar-playing, lyrics and Harp together formed a body of work that aroused an entire generation.

Practice a strong and clear **'Oy-yoy-yoy'** articulation. You may want to re-read Section X's discussion of tongue position for what I jokingly refer to as the 'Jewish' effect. Try to change the sound of the four and five suck chord as much as possible with each **'Yoy'**.

Remember to cut off the third **'Yoy'** after ½ beat and hold the next Blow note for 1½ beats. See if you can hit the three suck singly, but if not, at least move to the left for a three and four suck chord.

Lick A

oy — $\frac{45}{S}$ yoy — $\frac{45}{S}$ yoy — $\frac{45}{S}$ $\frac{45}{B}$ $\frac{3}{S}$ ...   oy — $\frac{45}{S}$ yoy — $\frac{45}{S}$ yoy — $\frac{45}{S}$ $\frac{45}{B}$ $\frac{34}{S}$ ...

½ beat   1½ beat

'Lick B' is a 16 beat version of our 8 beat 'Lick A'. We'll take the first 4 beats of 'Lick A' (oy-yoy-yoy-Blow) and repeat it twice, then tack on an entire 'Lick A'. Just as we combined two two-beat licks with a 4 beat lick to obtain an 8 beat lick in Section IX, we'll combine two four-beaters plus an eight-beater to get a 16 beat lick here.

Lick B

oy $\frac{45}{S}$ yoy $\frac{45}{S}$ yoy $\frac{45}{S}$ $\frac{45}{B}$ oy $\frac{45}{S}$ yoy $\frac{45}{S}$ yoy $\frac{45}{S}$ $\frac{45}{B}$ oy $\frac{45}{S}$ yoy $\frac{45}{S}$ yoy $\frac{45}{S}$ $\frac{45}{B}$ $\frac{3}{S}$ ...

We can play either 'Lick A' or 'Lick B' throughout a 12 Bar Verse. Make sure that you begin on the very first beat of the verse, and plug 6 'Lick A's' or 3 'Lick B's' into each verse. Actually, for variety, **I like to use both A and B in the same verse, as illustrated on the tape. Add a one suck Turnaround and you're in business! Listen to my 12 Bar Version a few times, and then try it yourself.**

You can either play along with my example (the vocal instructions may help), or use Steve's slower 12 Bar backing at the end of side B of the tape. With a bit of practice, you'll probably enjoy playing along with the faster backing even more.

'Dylanesque'

Tonic   ½ beat 1½ beat

Subdominant   Tonic

Dom.   Subd.   Tonic   Turnaround

John Lennon Style Jamming

Once you've mastered Licks A and B, try making up variations of your own using mid-range oy-yoy-yoy Sucks with a few Blow notes thrown in. The late and cruelly missed John Lennon, for instance, played a lick slightly similar to these on the Beatle's song 'I Should Have Known Better!' John repeats this lick (not on the tape) throughout the song, sometimes with a 'shake' of the four and five suck chords. In the original, he is using a 'C' harp (playing in the key of 'G')!

```
  oy        yoy
  4̇5   45   5̇6 56 5̇6        4̇5   45   5̇6 56 5̇6
  ~~   ~~                    ~~   ~~
  S    S    B  S  B          S    S    B  S  B
```

You might choose to make a 16 beat version out of it (somewhat like the Dylan Lick B) that might look like this (not on the tape) — Bounce it!

```
  oy   yoy                  oy   yoy                 oy   yoy
  4̇5  45  5̇6 56 5̇6  45  45  5̇6 56 5̇6  45  45  4̇5 45 4̇5 34...
  S   S   B  S  B   S   S   B  S  B   S   S   B  S  B  S
```

84

The Suck/Blow/Suck Jamming Patterns

I'm quite proud of myself for 'discovering' this method of teaching Blues Harp improvisation. It's so simple technically! If you can just learn to relax and let both the breath and music flow naturally, you'll be able to Jamm freely and creatively right away. And no worries about single notes here - chords work perfectly.

The crucial element now is **rhythm.** Listen over and over to my discussion of the 4 beat breathing pattern, while tapping your foot. You must Suck in **exactly** as your foot hits the floor, and Blow out forcefully and rapidly as your foot lifts, then be ready to Suck in again **exactly** as your foot hits the floor again. **Here's your four beat Suck/Blow/Suck pattern on a low chord:**

123 123 123 123 123 .   123 123 123 123 123 .
 S   B   S   B   S   S   B   S   B   S

Emphasize those downbeats (Sucks) by holding them a tiny bit longer than the Blows. This means that each Blow will have to last a bit shorter than each Suck. Make sure that each time your foot hits the floor - you inhale! And remember, the fourth beat of each bar is silent in this pattern.

Having any trouble with that 'emphasized downbeat' rhythm? Then pretend for a moment that the pattern is 12 beats long instead of four. It's easier to hear that way. Once you've mastered the rhythm as a 12 beater, go back to the original (and more useful) four beater, and it will seem much easier. **Here's the 12 beat simplified practice pattern. (The large dots indicate the 'real' beat):**

123 123 123 123 123 ..•..   123 123 123 123 123 ..•..
 S   B   S   B   S   S   B   S   B   S

Practice the four beat Suck/Blow/Suck rhythm without your Harp, with your mouth open to either single note or chord position. Memorize that rhythm.

$$\overset{\frown}{Suck}\ Blow\ \overset{\frown}{Suck}\ Blow\ Suck\ \bullet$$

Once you've gotten this breathing rhythm well fixed in your mind, move the Harp around in relation to your mouth while you breathe the memorized Suck/Blow/Suck rhythm.

You can use single notes or chords, although i feel that chords tend to sound better for this style of playing. I'll notate the licks (for my own convenience) as though we were single noting - but play them as chordally as you please.

Start with your mouth centered around the five suck and move one hole lower with each beat as you breathe the rhythm:

$$\overset{\frown}{5}\ \overset{\frown}{5}\ \overset{\frown}{4}\ \overset{\frown}{4}\ 3\ \bullet\ \overset{\frown}{5}\ \overset{\frown}{5}\ \overset{\frown}{4}\ \overset{\frown}{4}\ 3\ \bullet$$
$$S\ B\ S\ B\ S\ \quad\ S\ B\ S\ B\ S$$

Maintaining the rhythm is of crucial importance, so make sure that you can do it without having to think much about it. Now move that Harmonica around to your 'Harp's content'. **Start low and work your way up higher:**

$$\overset{\frown}{3}\ \overset{\frown}{4}\ \overset{\frown}{4}\ \overset{\frown}{5}\ 5\ \bullet\ \overset{\frown}{3}\ \overset{\frown}{4}\ \overset{\frown}{4}\ \overset{\frown}{5}\ 5\ \bullet$$
$$S\ B\ S\ B\ S\ \quad\ S\ B\ S\ B\ S$$

The above lick would work just as well had you started on one suck or five suck instead of three suck, that's the beauty of the Suck/Blow/Suck technique! **Once you've got the breathing rhythm, almost any notes will sound good!**

Start very high and work your way lower, with lots of sliding and saliva. I won't even bother to notate this type of lick as the variations are endless. Listen to my two examples, and make up some of your own.

Try moving it just a little, like from hole two to hole three, or from hole two to hole one:

$$2\overline{2}\ \overline{2\ 2}\ 3\ .\ \overline{2\ 2}\ \overline{2\ 2}\ 1\ .$$

S B S B S   S B S B S

The 8 Beat Suck/Blow/Suck Rhythm

Practice this rhythm pattern until it's really stuck in your head and lips. Tap your foot, and truly feel in your gut just how long those 8 beats last. Do it with the Harp (on your low chord at first) and empty-mouthed:

$$....\ \underline{1\dot{2}3}\ \underline{1\dot{2}3}\ \underline{1\dot{2}3}\ \underline{1\dot{2}3}\ \underline{1\dot{2}3}\ \underline{1\dot{2}3}\ \underline{1\dot{2}3}\ \underline{1\dot{2}3}\ \underline{1\dot{2}3}\ \underline{1\dot{2}3}\ \underline{1\dot{2}3}\ \underline{1\dot{2}3}\ \underline{1\dot{2}3}\ .$$

S   B   S   B   S   B   S   B   S   B   S   B   S

Use this 8 beat pattern to go from five suck down towards one suck and then back up to five suck. Or go all the way from the high end to the low end, or low to high. Listen to my illustrations on the tape. **I haven't notated these because I don't want you thinking about exactly which holes you're landing on. It doesn't matter as long as you maintain the proper breathing rhythm with the Suck notes on the downbeats.**

2:61

Taking It Through a 12 Bar

I like to use a 16 beat breathing rhythm in my 12 Bars, which I create by adding an eight-beater to two four-beaters. **Give your 12 Bar some structural help by taking the rhythm up high for the Dominant and ending your rhythm on a one Suck for your Turnaround.** That's all you really need to know!

For you analytically minded folk, I'll describe my two (slow and fast) demonstration 12 Bars. Read my description while you listen to the verses six or eight times, and perhaps you'll gain some ideas for your own playing.

In the slower verse, my First Tonic begins with two four-beat rhythms that go from five to three, followed by an eight-beater that runs five to one and back to five. The next 16 beats (First Subdominant and Second Tonic) are almost the same, with a few extra slide-sucks up to the initial five sucks. Then I slide (while Sucking) to get way up high for the Dominant, work my way slowly down in the eight beats of Dominant and Second Subdominant, and do a fancy Third Tonic: five to three to five then down to one for a Turnaround. Sound complicated? Easier done than read about!

My second and faster 12 Bar illustration uses four and eight beat breathing rhythms that move mostly between five and three, and occasionally down to one. I go up high for my Dominant, and finally break away from the expected rhythm to tack on a five suck to one suck turnaround.

These types of 12 Bars are easier played than read about - don't think so much! Now is the time to use the relaxation/visualization exercise, and knock out some 'gut-level' 12 Bars of Suck/Blow/Suck rhythms along with Steve's guitar backing.

Last Licks: Our Two Beat Suck/Blow/Suck Rhythm

This two beat breathing rhythm is quite different from the others. **It begins on an upbeat, and one of the Blow notes falls on a downbeat:**

one two 123 123 123 123 123 .. 123 123 123 123 123 ..
       S   B   S   B   S   S   B   S   B   S

Now sandwich your new breathing rhythm into the breaks of the 'I'm a Person' lick:

.. 2432 123 123 123 123 123 2432 123 123 123 123 123
   SBSS S   B   S   B   S SBSS S   B   S   B   S

2432 55443 2432 slide 77777 and so on ...
SBSS SBSBS SBSS   SBSBS

Like that? Then go back to the Boogie guitar backing in Section XI and jamm some!

Visualization, Relaxation, and 'Playing from the Gut'

For many of us, it's difficult to create music spontaneously, without conscious thought. If we have doubts about our musical abilities, free improvisation may seem like a hopelessly optimistic goal. Yet I believe that we all posess an internal reservoir of talent, if we can only learn to tap it's hidden depth.

As I've already expressed in my section on "Zen and the Art of Blues Harp Blowing," improvised music flows from a very special 'place'. A psycho-physiologist would probably prefer to label this 'place' as the **'right hemisphere of the brain'**. A martial artist would call it the **'hara'** or **'one-point'**, and a hypnotist the **'self-induced trance'.** The Zen monk might know such a space as **'mushin'** or **'no-mind',** while the Southern Blues musician would advise you to **'play from your gut!'**

However **you** might choose to label this point from which improvised music flows most freely - this exercise will help you to locate it.

Sit comfortably in a warm, quiet, room. Make sure that your Harmonica and tape deck are within easy reach, and that your tape casette is positioned to the Jamming 12 Bars near the end of Side Two.

Tighten the muscles of your feet and hold them tensely for a second or two. Relax them. Do this once more. Travel upward through your body, tensing and relaxing, tensing and relaxing each muscle group. Calves, thighs, behind, stomach, chest, shoulders, arms, hands, neck, jaw and eyes. Then relax your entire body as completely as you can. Concentrate on feeling warm and heavy, warm and heavy. Say 'warm and heavy' to yourself as you tense and relax.

Now picture your body becoming filled up with a clear, luminous light or fluid. Let it flow through your feet, then up into your legs and trunk and head until it suffuses your entire being. Take as long as you like to picture this happening, **But try to visualize it as realistically as possible.** If your mind tends to wander (it may at first, especially if you are unaccustomed to such exercises), return your attention to the inflowing luminous fluid as quickly and completely as you can, as soon as you notice that you've wandered.

The deeper your relaxation, and the clearer your image or visualization of the luminous fluid - the more effective this type of technique (used by many Olympic Athletes) can be. Many people find that listening to the Jamming 12 Bars (and the accompanying subliminal suggestions) **during** the relaxation and visualization process helps to achieve a stronger effect with less effort. The only drawback to doing so is that you will have to rewind the tape before proceeding with the rest of the exercise.

Now that you're completely relaxed and 'luminescent', you can use this altered state of consciousness in two ways.

A. Turn on the Jamming 12 Bars, and just visualize the luminous fluid flowing out of you, through your Harp, and producing beautiful, exciting Blues music along with Steve's guitar backing or:

B. Turn on the cassette 12 Bars, and put your Harp to your mouth (using slow, dreamy, movements that don't reduce your relaxation). Picture the luminous fluid flowing through your Harp as you play **anything** that you like. **Try not to think at all about what you're playing.** But if you **must** do something 'planned,' use a simple and general rule like the Tonic Jamming Rule or the Suck/Blow/Suck Rule, and think as little as possible once you've decided upon the general rule that you'll be using to improvise with.

The more familiar and comfortable you are with the basic techniques and styles of playing that I've included in my instructions, the more options you will have at your disposal when you put your brain on 'automatic pilot' and 'play from your gut!'

You'll find that when you're ready to return to the so-called 'real' world, just take a few deep Harmonica - player's breaths, stretch, and rise up feeling rested, energetic, and musical!

Steve's Guitar Backing

Every Harpist needs an 'on call' Blues guitarist! If you're not lucky enough to have a live one, this part of the tape will help. Here we have Steve playing two sets of 12 Bars to play along with. One is medium speed, the other faster. I've 'embedded' a series of subliminal (beneath the consciously audible level) suggestions into these backing 12 Bars. The suggestions will help you to relax, think positively about your musical abilities, and not be too self-critical. This portion of the tape could possibly relax you too much to be safely used while driving, especially if you are tired to start with.

If you like the sound of Blues Guitar, or harbor a fantasy of playing Harp and Guitar a la Bob Dylan, you might be interested in my **Instant Guitar Cassette Program.** It's aimed at total beginners and especially those who have tried before without success.

I'm not much of a Blues Guitarist, but I like to play a few 12 Bars for my Harp classes. So after a number of students requested Guitar lessons, I had to turn my thoughts in that direction. And, following considerable experimentation, I'm almost ready to unveil my new cassette program. I believe that it's the easiest Guitar Learning Method ever, and many students are pickin' out simple Blues and Folk songs within an hour!

If you play some already, this isn't for you. But if you're a total beginner and can beg, borrow, or steal a functioning 'gitbox' for an afternoon, see my offer on page 109!

'Rack'

92

Singin' The Blues

There's no reason why you shouldn't start singing along with Blues, no matter how bad you think your voice is. Just do it privately at first, or with friends while drinking (a few drinks will reduce your own vocal inhibitions and soften the critical faculties of said comrades). Playing Harp will eventually improve your voice (mine went from awful to merely mediocre in less than a year).

There is one very common way to fit the line of a song into a 12 Bar Blues. It's called the A-A-B pattern, because each verse consists of three lines, with the first two lines almost the same (A) and the third line different, but rhyming on the last word (B).

Since we're fitting 3 lines into 12 Bars, each line can occupy 4 Bars. We usually have a break that is a few beats long in the middle of each line, and a few beats after each vocal line to put Harmonica **'Fills'** in. Often the first word of the first line of the verse doesn't begin on the first beat of the verse (as one might expect). Instead that first word 'anticipates' the verse by beginning on the last beat of the previous 12 Bar. Listen to my example (a song is worth a thousand words). And of course, feel free to play your Harp over, along with, or in the breaks of my deathless lyrics...

(well if) trouble was water ·· I would be a divin' fool ······
    ⌐→ First tonic

I said if trouble was water ·· Dave Harp would be a divin' fool ······
    ⌐→ First Subd.   ⌐→ Second Tonic

He just might climb up a fifty foot tower ·· And dive into a six foot pool ······
    ⌐→ Dominant   Subdominant   ⌐→Third tonic

© Dave Harp 1984

Now think up two rhyming words of your own, and an idea that connects them, and try to make a Blues verse of your own, in exactly the same format as above. Listen to some Blues singers for inspiration!

Open Harp Surgery:

I'll go into harmonica repair in greater detail in Volume Two, as your Harp shouldn't be having any 'age-related' problems yet. But if one day a note should sound buzzy, fuzzy, or just won't make any sound; try this. Gently remove with key or butterknife (by prying as they're only held on by little rivets) the appropriate cover plate (Suck Notes bottom plate; Blow notes top plate) and look closely at the problematic reed. **Anything big enough to keep the reed from sounding is big enough to see and remove!** A hair, thread, or piece of unidentifiable dried food is the most common culprit, caught between reed and casing. Use a pin or thin piece of wire to push a Blow reed down from outside or a Suck reed up from inside to free the debris. **Always try Blowing and Sucking a stuck hole to free it before you open it up.** Just use your tongue as a block to avoid inhaling old lint or potato chippette!

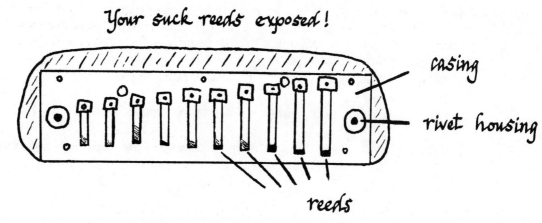

Your suck reeds exposed!

casing

rivet housing

reeds

What About Other Key Harps?

Each key Harp is different, excitingly so. 'G' is usually the lowest, and 'F#' the highest. I've learned from extensive research with my student 'guinea pigs' that people progress fastest (especially in learning the Bending techniques) if they work with **both** a high and a low Harp. **In Volume Two we'll use an 'A' Harp.** Having two Harps is like having two pairs of shoes to wear in that each Harp feels a bit different and that both last much longer if you alternate their use. So get an 'A' if you crave another already, eventually you'll probably want to own a variety of keys and types.

Discography:

Although listening to the great harpists on records is very important; I believe that it's not a bad idea to wait for a few weeks and absorb the material in this package before trying to learn from the recorded Masters. Once you understand **Bending** and **Deviant Blues Structures** (Volume II) you'll find the material on Blues records much more accessible to you.

I'll include an extensive discography in Volume II, with the correct Harp for each song listed. However, if you'd like to know the names of a few of my favorite Harpists (many of their records are available in new and used record stores), here they are (in no particular order):

Sonny Terry, Little Walter, Jimmy Reed, Sonny Boy Williamson (number I or II), Big Walter Horton, Norton Buffalo, Paul Butterfield, John Mayall, James Cotton, Huey Lewis, J. Geils, Lee Oskar and Muddy Waters (not a Harpist but a Bandleader who features Harp) — you can't go wrong with any of these folk. And don't forget Big Mama Thornton, one of the few female Harmonicists. Women have traditionally tended to avoid playing professional Blues Harp — let's start changing that right now (practice, sisters)!

Playing Along With Records And Other People

If you already have a Blues record and want to play along with it, first try to identify the songs that have a 12 Bar or Boogie structure. Then see if your two suck note or chord sounds 'right' when played throughout the Boogie, or during the Tonic Sections of the 12 Bar (you'll be able to tell if it doesn't). If it does, then the song is in the right 'key' for your 'F' Harp. If not, then you won't be able to play along with the song (if your turntable has 'pitch control', you can try to adjust it to make your two suck fit - it's worth a try).

Some records (like John Mayall's for example) list the key of each song on the album cover. Or perhaps you have a musician friend with guitar or piano who can 'key' a favorite album for you. If you can discover the key of a song and are willing to buy a new Harp, here is a chart which indicates which key Harp goes with which key Blues. As we know, our 'F' Harp plays best with a 'C' Blues.

Want to jamm with other musicians? Make sure that you have the right key Harp for the Blues key that they're playing in (check the chart). If they're not playing a Blues, you still may be able to play along if you have the right key harp.

Cross Harp Chart

Blues Key:	C	D♭	D	E♭	E	F	G♭	G	A♭	A	B♭	B	C
Harp to Use:	F	F♯	G	A♭	A	B♭	B	C	D♭	D	E♭	E	F

Some Respect and Support:

Although I enjoy and respect the contributions of the many excellent young American and British Blues or Rock Bands, I feel that in these days of publicity hype and media overkill it is often easy to overlook the original people and culture that gave us the Blues music. I've been blessed with the ability to communicate and convey information clearly, but I'm also very aware that my contribution rests entirely upon the shoulders of the Bluesmen and Blueswomen that came before.

So if any of those original Bluespeople come your way — catch their shows, buy their records, go up to them after a show and shake their hands — they've given us more than we can repay.

I received the letter below after a Benefit concert for J.C. and an Oakland California Elementary school. J.C. Burris is Sonny Terry's nephew (he was Sonny's 'seeing eye kid' for a while in the 1920's & 30's). Now J.C. may be the world's finest Solo Country Blues Harpist!

JC BURRIS

Date oct. 12, 1981

Dear Dave,

your music was loud but e really want to thank you for helping our concert being good. Your music was good but loud e also want to thank you for making our concert a success. and bringing J.C. Burris to our concert, e think J.C. was a little better than you. The only reason is because he had put puppets in his act. and also because J.C. is a very old blues harmonica player.

your friend,
Ozisha

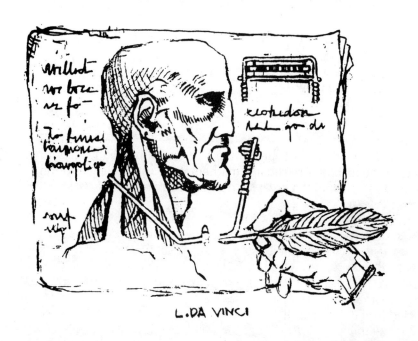

L. DA VINCI

If you look deeply enough into anything,
you can learn something about everything.

The Scale of The Universe

Many people consider music to be just a pleasant diversion or at most a popular art form, but fortunately Pythagoras was not one of these narrow minded folk. For the form and structure of music appear to be reflections of the entire universe, from atom to galaxy.

The Greeks used ratio theory (the science of the mathematical relationships of one thing to another) with great success in many different disciplines. Ratios determined the idealized physical proportions of the human body, so that the length of a statue's head had a particular mathematical ratio relative to the length of the body, and the girth of the arms bore a specific relationship to that of the legs. But Pythagoras was not merely grinding his favorite theoretical axe when he applied mathematical ratios to the distances between notes. I say this because the musical notes that he obtained and the ratios that he used to produce them have a far, far wider application than he knew (or did he?). Strangely enough, even though other cultures have scales of vastly varying size and complexity (the Chinese scale has 5 notes and the East Indian 22), many of the notes used in **all** cultures are the same. It's possible that this amazingly widespread usage of certain notes is due "only" to the psychological and physical properties that all human beings have in common. But this explanation, based as it is on the **human** experience, cannot begin to explain why Pythagoras' ratio itself (not just the notes) appears to possess an awesome universality. For it seems that both the ratio of the distances between the sun and the planets of the solar system, and the ratio of the distances between the quantum levels of energy in the molecule bear a strong similarity to - you guessed it - the ratios used by Pythagoras in determining scale structure.

Perhaps we human beings are just unlucky enough to be **The Wrong Size** to appreciate the flabbergastingly high degree of unity in all of creation. But although I can scarcely keep my desk top in order, I am proud to be even a small, disorganized part of what I consider to be "God's mind."

Harperobics™

There's only one musical instrument that can be played with one hand (or none) while inhaling and exhaling. And that, of course, is the reason that cowboys and sailors were never known as tuba players or flautists. As I've said elsewhere, it is probably easier to play Harp while walking than it is to play while merely tapping your foot, since your stride provides you with a natural 'swing' beat!

If you enjoy walking, jogging, hiking or biking — incorporate some Harp into your favorite outdoors exercise. You'll find that Harpin' at the same time will increase your aerobic workout! Runners will achieve a 'runner's high' sooner, and long distance walkers and bikers will find time and distance passing faster.

I've been working with some students who suffer from respiratory disabilities, and the preliminary results are promising. So if you have any asthmatic or emphysemic friends, you might encourage them to consider 'Harmonica Therapy'. Speaking of disabilities, the Harp is also ideal for people who lack manual agility. I have a few quadriplegic students who use 'Dylan-style' racks to hold their Harps!

Commuters, cabbies, salespeople and others who drive a lot find the harp a wonderful way to avoid boredom on the road. With a tape deck and my cassette, every traffic jam can become a 'Jamm Session!'

Super-Harperobics™

Although walking and playing is fun, if you are involved with any other types of athletics you may want to incorporate your Harp into them as well. Every year a group of students run the San Francisco Bay to Breakers Race (7.62 miles) with me, playing all the way. Sound impressive? It's really not that difficult. Just concentrate on 'recycling' that breath through the Harmonica, and revert to a train if you can't think of anything else to do! You have to Blow and Suck anyways, so why not get some music out of it, too...

On distances over a mile or two most 'Harp-runners' find that a 'rack' (available in any music store for under $5.00) allows them to swing their arms more freely and comfortably. But a few prefer merely to alternate hands every few hundred yards.

I've recently begun to Blow in more esoteric situations, and I'd like to encourage you to do the same. Here are a few of my favorite 'Harp-sports'.

Skiing: Choose an easy downhill run and leave your poles at the bottom. Concentrate on rhythm as you gently cut back and forth. Beats the heck out of a Sony Walkman, for my money!

Hiking: Playing in the pure mountain air is a real turn-on for me! How high can you get? Make sure that your lungs are in good shape before you try blowing at altitudes over 4,000 feet - the air really thins out up there. 14,000 feet is my limit so far, but I'm workin' on it! Pay special attention to other camper's and hikers 'audial privacy' especially at night, though...

Kayaking: Duct-tape a Harp to the center of your paddle, and play river songs as you 'go with the flow'. This one is a real crowd pleaser, and easy if you don't try it during a rapid!

Fishing, Sailing, Bicycling — the list goes on and on. If you have a favorite 'Harp-pastime', write and tell me about it. I love to hear from fellow **'harmonomaniacs!'**

Harp Etiquette Hints

Be sensitive to other people's reactions to your playing, especially in quiet or enclosed spaces. Learn to play softly, almost inaudibly, especially in the library or church. Play in the street, but **not** at 2 a.m. Most people will enjoy your music, but remember: Be considerate, since you represent the proud order of Harmonicists now!

Bibliography:

As far as I know, the definitive biography of the Blues Harp and it's many and varied adherents has yet to be written (a future project for me, perhaps?). However, if you are interested in obtaining more 'already' written music, any good music store should have a number of Harmonica songbooks which use notation not tremendously different (though less clear, I believe) from mine. Otherwise, I merely advise you to grab good old Volume Two of this epic project (which is already plugged elsewhere nearby).

If you are interested in the Zen or relaxation/visualization aspects of my book, I strongly recommend Stephen Levine's "A Gradual Awakening" (Anchor Press, 1979) or "Who Dies?" (Anchor Press 1982). If I were in the market for a guru, he'd probably be it...

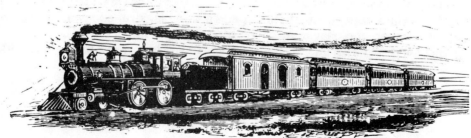

Moneyback Guarantee:

I'm so confident that my package can teach anyone to play some Harp if properly used that I'm willing to put my money where my mouth (and, coincidentally, my Harmonica)is!

So: If your first look-through of my book and listen-through of my cassette does not convince you on the spot that you'll probably get your money's worth out of it (and I personally think that the understanding of the Blues Scale and Structure alone is cheap at $12.95), then do the following:

On a tape cassette record me five minutes of your practicing every week for a month. If at the end of the month you don't feel that you've made any progress; mail me your tape along with my book and tape in good condition. If somehow you are not using the package correctly — and that will be easier to judge if you include a few weekly comments on problems or sticking points — I'll send you a personal letter to set you straight. If through some inadequacy of mine you're having trouble, well, then my check will be in the return mail; and I'll work hard to clarify the rough spot in my next edition. Fair enough?

Special Free Offer

I was recently invited to present short instructional lectures at the 'West Coast Harmonica Summits', which featured Paul Butterfield, James Cotton, and Norton Buffalo (3 of the finest—fun to hang out with, too!). The concerts were endorsed by the M. Hohner Company, and consequently I am the proud owner of two crates of beautiful, full color, slightly dated (1982), Harmonica Calendars, which I offer to you **free** (while supply lasts). Twelve suitable-for-framing photos! Please check out the order form on page 109.

Dear Students:

As you may have already guessed, dear students, I am not one of your enormous multinational corporations with an advertising budget equal to the Gross National Product of the average Third World state.

So, since I cannot afford to buy large chunks of TV time, or direct mail to every home in the country, I must ask **you** to help spread the word by **word of mouth** technique. It's the most sincere and reliable advertising method, anyways! I thank you in advance for telling your friends, neighbors, family (one family in Washington state has bought books for father, daughter, and 2 sons already!) and even interested passers-by on the street about my product. I truly believe that almost anybody's life can be made more satisfying through creative self-expression on the Blues Harp!

If you agree, please help me out with some free publicity. Does your local music, gift, or outdoors retailer carry this package? If not, you might mention it to them. By the way, I'm not too shy about asking this because: A) I have great faith in my product, B) I can use the business, and C) **The more folk Blow, the more there are to Jamm with!**

Blowing your own horn isn't always so easy by yourself.
—Dave Harp

Sales Pitch

If you're enjoying this package, I have a few other items that you might like as well. You'll find that once you open yourself to music with the Harmonica, learning other instruments is easy, too!

Instant Tin Flute for the Musical Idiot!

This amazingly simple Flute book will teach you Folk, Blues, Classical, Country and Traditional Irish music on the Tin Flute, using my original notation system (similar to Harptab™). May be even easier to learn than Harmonica! Package includes top-quality Tin Flute for only $9.95, plus $1.00 postage and handling.

Instant Guitar for the Musical Idiot! (And 'Kids' Harp)

Once again, a highly original and unique teaching method that insures near instant results! See page 92 for further details. This package will be more cassette than book, and publication is planned for late 1984. Pre-publication price only $10.00, post-paid. My 'Instant Folk and Blues Harp for Kid s' should be available around then, too. That'll cost $14.95 for book, cassette, and Harp.

60 Minute Jamming Tape

Lots of fun for your 'F' Harp! Guitar and Piano backing in a variety of styles. Only $8 post-paid.

Golden Melody F

Need a harp for <u>this</u> package? Send $12.50 post-paid for a new Golden Melody F, $7.00 for Silvertone Deluxe.

Free Photo-Calendar

Send me $1.00 to cover postage and handling, and you'll get twelve full color photos of famous Harmonicists (including Sonny Terry, Lee Oskar, and Fingers Taylor) attractively packaged in a 1982 Hohner calendar.

Mailing List

Would you like to be on my mailing list, and recieve information about new products, Harmonica events, and gossip? Then send a stamped, self-addressed envelope!

Cash, check, or C.O.D. orders accepted. Add $1.00 for First Class delivery if you're in a rush!

Volume II

The mysterious Volume II that I've been shamelessly plugging throughout my package is a direct continuation of this book and tape. **It's not an 'advanced' text, suitable only for the most serious students. In fact, the easier parts of Volume II are simpler to play than the harder parts of Volume I, and many of the Volume II songs and licks can be played using chords if you haven't mastered single notes yet.** Many students find that listening to Volume II while they are still working with Volume I helps them to see what they are 'aiming for', Harmonica - wise!

Volume II will take many of our Volume I licks and 12 Bars, and add new techniques and refinements to them. It will offer new songs and Harp-styles such as Country and Western style, Hard Rock (J. Geils-style), Sonny Terry-style Harp, Norton Buffalo-style Harp, and Chicago-style playing. The Hows and Whens of Bending will be covered simply but exhaustively. More tips on playing with bands, records, and other people will be offered to help you feel comfortable when Jamming.

And there will be lots more backing-music (by a full electric Blues Band) to play along with!

So if I've convinced you to grab a Volume II, all you have to do is send $12.95 postpaid to me. Need a Golden Melody 'A' for your Volume II? Add a mere $10 (offer good with book/tape only), or $5 for a Silvertone Deluxe 'A'.

David Harp
Box 187
3309½ Mission Street
San Francisco, CA 94110

We live on one planet,
with one life support system.
The survival of all humanity,
all life, is totally interdependent.

Dear David:

"What Fun! Has literally changed my life—which wasn't so bad before harmonica! An excellent presentation."
                                                                    M.S. III, Oakland, CA

"I learned more (from Dave's method) than in five years of college."   J.B., San Francisco, CA

"My lips are chapped and my cheeks are sore but send Volume Two anyway...a grateful idiot,"
                                                                    E.C., Oakland, CA

"You're the Harmonica Guru - I 'got it' in one day!"   B.G., Tavanier, FL

"I am nearly thru Volume One and I have thoroughly enjoyed it, not to mention my Harmonica abilities have improved immensely. My seven year old son Colby has also become addicted, and has surprised me with his ability to understand your musical notation."
                                                                    T.L., Berkeley, CA

"Bought one for myself, brother, sister, and now father."   T.J. Mercer Island, WA

"OK, I'm hooked. Send me volume II fast. I need another fix."   J.C., Oakland, CA

"This is an excellent teaching system. I've tried to learn the Harp from other people and various methods with no success. Now I'm well on my way to feeling secure about my increasing ability to play the Harp. Thanks."
                                                                    P.C., Chapel Hill, NC

"I thoroughly enjoyed Volume I of 'Blues Harmonica for the Musical Idiot'. I'm no longer an 'Idiot' but am more crazy than ever about the Blues. You done good!"   M.S.P. MD, Thermopolis, WY

"A hearty handshake, a pat on the back, and sincerest thanks for providing your books for 'Musical Developmentally Disadvantaged' children such as I. Oh frabjous joy!"   J.W., Anchorage, AK

The above quotations are all taken from actual unsolicited letters received recently, and represent the types of comments that occur most frequently. Many of my customers go on to buy my Tin Flute package and gift copies of my Harmonica book in addition to the excitedly-awaited 'Volume II'.